The Establishment and Use of Dedicated Taxes for Health

World Health Organization
Regional Office for the Western Pacific
2004

Acknowledgements

This report was written for WHO by Ms Addy Carol, former Executive Director of the Western Australia Health Promotion Foundation (Healthway). This work was made possible through extrabudgetary contribution to the World Health Organization by the Government of Japan.

WHO Library Cataloguing in Publication Data

The establishment and use of dedicated taxes for health.

1. Health promotion. 2. Taxes. 3. Tobacco industry -- economics.

ISBN 92 9061 171 5 (NLM Classification: WA 525)

Publications of the World Health Organization can be obtained from Marketing and Dissemination, World Health Organization, 20 Avenue Appia, 1211 Geneva 27, Switzerland (tel: +41 22 791 2476; fax: +41 22 791 4857; email: bookorders@who.int). Requests for permission to reproduce WHO publications, in part or in whole, or to translate them – whether for sale or for noncommercial distribution – should be addressed to Publications, at the above address (fax: +41 22 791 4806; email: permissions@who.int). For WHO Western Pacific Regional Publications, request for permission to reproduce should be addressed to Publications Office, World Health Organization, Regional Office for the Western Pacific, P.O. Box 2932, 1000, Manila, Philippines, Fax. No. (632) 521-1036, email: publications@wpro.who.int

Table of Contents

PREFACE

Funding for prevention of unnecessary death and disease has always been a challenge for those involved in public health. This is particularly evident in the case of tobacco control. No one likes to pay more taxes, especially when governments invariably raise taxes on recreational products like alcohol and tobacco. However, the evidence presented in this report shows significant community support when, if taxes are increased, the additional tax is used to educate and enhance the health and well-being of the population.

Tobacco use will not change rapidly and will continue to be a challenge for years to come. However, the adoption of the Framework Convention on Tobacco Control (FCTC) at the 2003 World Health Assembly has set the stage for development of policies and allocation of funding to implement the various aspects of the treaty. Article 26 of the FCTC provides for a contribution from each party or Member State to implement national activities aimed at controlling tobacco and to assist in meeting the treaty obligations and requirements outlined. This document suggests a way for many countries to achieve both of these objectives.

For many years, ministries of finance have not looked favourably on the idea of designating or hypothecating funding from tagged taxes on tobacco or other products. However, this attitude is now changing, and examples of the processes and background to such change are clearly outlined in this report. Health and finance ministries may use this documentation as a guide to follow the examples of the Republic of Korea, Switzerland, Thailand or other countries with designated taxes. It is one clear way in which health and other ministries can collaborate to enhance health in the Western Pacific Region.

Shigeru Omi

Shigeru Omi, M.D., Ph.D.
Regional Director
WHO Regional Office for the Western Pacific

1 INTRODUCTION

1.1 Background to the report

Since the mid 1980s, governments in a number of countries and states have agreed to dedicate part of their tax revenues for particular health promotion initiatives. These funds have been variously described as dedicated, hypothecated or tagged taxes.

They have tended to come from such sources as alcohol, tobacco or gambling, the so-called 'sin' taxes. In some cases they have been used to fund general health promotion activities, while in others they have been used to specifically address problems in the area from which the tax was derived.

The allocation of such taxes for health promotion activities has required new and innovative approaches, which have led to the development of new and innovative methods to administer and allocate the funds. In the past decade, there has been a steady increase in the number of states and countries introducing these methods in order to fund health promotion /tobacco control programmes.

The Framework Convention on Tobacco Control (FCTC), which is the world's first global agreement devoted entirely to tobacco control, has the potential to act as a further catalyst for countries and states wishing to expand their health promotion activities, particularly in working to actively curb the use of tobacco. A number of obligations contained in the treaty may be directly addressed through dedicated taxes and directing funds to tobacco control.

Relevant obligations include:

- Price and tax measures: implementing tax policies and, where appropriate, price policies "so as to contribute to the health objectives aimed at reducing tobacco consumption".

- Advertising, promotion and sponsorship: "Each party shall, in accordance with its constitutional principles, undertake a comprehensive ban on all tobacco advertising, promotion and sponsorship".
- Education, communication, training and public awareness: "Each party shall promote and strengthen public awareness of tobacco control issues, using all available communication tools as appropriate." [1]

The requirement to finance public health campaigns and other aspects of tobacco control, which is implicit in the obligations proposed by the FCTC, may be a concern for some countries, particularly developing countries. It is, therefore, timely to explore new and innovative methods of funding which have already been successfully implemented in a range of jurisdictions.

This report draws on the collective experiences of those countries and states which have introduced dedicated taxes for health promotion or tobacco control purposes. **It has been prepared with a view to providing support to WHO Member States and countries wishing to address the obligations contained in the treaty and /or undertake a range of other health promotion activities.**

1.2 Overview of the report

The report aims to document the history and scope of the use of dedicated taxes for health promotion. It provides a rationale for the introduction of tobacco taxes, some or all of which may be earmarked for health promotion activities. It highlights the processes, strategies and challenges involved, and also summarizes a number of examples of states and countries which have already gone down this track.

The different organizational structures for administering the dedicated funds are described, the underpinning rationales are outlined, and a summary of the advantages and disadvantages of each organizational model is provided. The report also examines legislative and governance considerations, and explores the challenging area of evaluating the organizations and their work.

Finally, the important role of the new funding organizations in tobacco control receives consideration, with a focus on the role they may play in the replacement of tobacco sponsorship.

---

[1] *Framework Convention on Tobacco Control.* Geneva, World Health Assembly, May 2003.

Methodology

Information was collected from a number of countries and states where dedicated taxes and organizational models to administer the funds have been introduced. Some 15 questionnaires were distributed to relevant organizations. Knowledge was gathered using the Internet and other written sources, as well as through personal contact.[2]

The International Network of Health Promotion Foundations generously provided further documentation. This group involves more than 10 health promotion foundations and represents one of the major new administrative models which have evolved.[3]

1.3 Parameters

The processes of introducing tobacco taxes, dedicating some or all of them for health promotion purposes, and then determining the organizational structure required to allocate the funds in a way which will bring optimal health benefits for the community, are inextricably linked. Advocates for dedicated taxes must be able to present a clear and firm vision, not only of the uses to which the funds are to be directed, but also of the mechanisms by which the funds will be allocated.

In discussing how and why to raise taxes for health promotion /tobacco control purposes, the report concentrates on tobacco taxes. **Readers should note that the principles, rationale and arguments used in the case of tobacco may be readily adapted and applied to other taxes, such as alcohol and gambling.**

Despite the important connection between the steps involved in establishing taxes, the dedication of all or part, and the establishment of an appropriate funding body for distribution to achieve health promotion gains, the report generally deals with them separately. However, there will be some overlap in terms of the rationale, evidence and processes involved.

The report is a synthesis of information gathered rather than examples of individual case studies. In exploring the stories of different states and countries, particularly in relation to the establishment of dedicated taxes, there is a paucity of formal documentation. Much of the information included is recalled by the key people involved at the time. Interestingly, many of the reported experiences, strategies and challenges were similar in a range of jurisdictions.

---

[2] To provide background for this report a postal survey was carried out to gather information and experiences from those states and countries that have already dedicated taxes for health promotion activities and established specific administrative structures to disburse the funds. Fifteen questionnaires were sent out, mainly to those involved in the International Health Promotion Network. There were 10 responses.

[3] The International Network of Health Promotion Foundations, established in 1999, currently has seven members and a number of associate members. Its mission is to strengthen the capacities of countries to promote the health of populations through health promotion foundations at national and subnational levels. For 2002-2004, Health Promotion Switzerland is responsible for the Secretariat (contact: ursel.broesskamp@promotionsante.ch).

It is important that readers recognize that the report does not claim to present an infallible recipe for success. It summarizes the experiences of various countries and states while providing a range of examples. Ideally, it will be used to develop practical tools and protocols that will suit the individual needs of countries and states after they have taken into account their prevailing political, social, economic and health-promoting environments.

2 TAXING TOBACCO

2.1 Why tax tobacco?

There are a number of excellent reasons for increasing tobacco tax and for doing so on a regular basis to at least match the rate of growth of incomes and ensure that cigarettes do not become more affordable. **Tax increases that substantially increase the retail price of cigarettes have been described as the most effective measure to reduce tobacco demand.**[4] Those countries which do not yet have tobacco taxes in place need to consider introducing such measures as a matter of urgency for the following reasons.

Higher prices reduce consumption

The major and most compelling reason for introducing tobacco taxes and regularly increasing them is to increase the price of tobacco to the smoker. This in turn reduces consumption, which means that increasing the price of cigarettes through raising taxation is the single most effective policy tool to decrease smoking.[5]

Economic theory suggests that, as the price of tobacco increases, demand for the product falls. Children, adolescents and people on low incomes are most responsive to increases in price, so the impact of the measure is greatest among those groups.[6]

It is estimated that a 10% price increase reduces overall consumption by 4% in developed countries and 8% in developing countries.[7]

[4] Jha P, Chaloupka F. The economics of global control. *British Medical Journal*, 2000, 7257; 358-361.
[5] *Curbing the epidemic. Governments and the economics of tobacco control.* Development in practice series. Washington, DC, World Bank, 1999:76,77.
[6] *Ibid*: 42.
[7] *Ibid*: 41.

In support of the initiative to increase tobacco tax in Thailand, projections of the effect of tax increases on cigarette sales, revenue and youth smoking indicated that a tax increase from the then current rate of 55% to 61% would prevent some 200 000 young people from smoking. A further increase to 63% would stop 30 ,000 young people from starting to smoke.[8]

Further evidence of the power of tax increases on demand for cigarettes is contained in a Philip Morris memo of 1993[9]

> "... the 1982-83 round of price increases caused two million adults to quit smoking and prevented 600 000 teenagers from starting to smoke.... We don't need to have that happen again."

Tax increases are a cost-effective measure

Tobacco taxes have been singled out as the most cost-effective intervention in relation to reducing tobacco consumption.[10] It is estimated that, depending on the assumptions made about the administrative cost of increasing and monitoring higher tobacco taxes, the cost of implementing a tax increase of 10% could be less than US$ 5 per disability–adjusted life year (DALY) and would be unlikely to be more than US$ 17 per DALY in low- to middle-income countries.[11]

There can be no doubt that actions that involve increasing tobacco taxes are clearly justified for a number of reasons.

"Policies that reduce demand for tobacco, such as the decision to increase tobacco taxes, will not cause long-term job losses in the vast majority of countries. Nor will higher tobacco taxes reduce tax revenues; rather, revenues would climb in the medium term. Such policies could, in sum, bring unprecedented health benefits without harming economies."[12]

An appropriate level of tobacco tax

Defining an appropriate level of tax is complex as it will depend upon a number of factors, including the degree to which the community wishes to protect children, as well as revenue considerations. As a useful yardstick it has been suggested that, where comprehensive tobacco control programmes are in place, the tax should be at least two-thirds to four-fifths of the retail price.[13]

[8] Ritthiphakdee Bung-on. *Tobacco taxation and dedicated tax; a win –win strategy for tobacco control. Thailand's experience*. Paper presented at the INB 5 Meeting, Geneva, 2002.
[9] PMDoc 2045447810, www.pmdocs.com
[10] World Bank. *Op cit*. Ref 5 :76,77.
[11] *Ibid*:77.
[12] *Ibid*: 2.
[13] Chaloupka F. Paper presented at the 2nd National Tobacco Conference, April 2003. Melbourne, Australia.

This section has highlighted the important reasons for governments to introduce and increase tobacco taxes in order to directly reduce consumption. The benefits to the community can be further increased if it is decided to dedicate all or part of the tax for specific health promotion /tobacco control initiatives and establish an appropriate organization and structure to allocate the funds.

2.2 Key steps to success

The importance of those countries that have not yet introduced tobacco taxes taking immediate steps to do so cannot be overemphasized.

The arguments stated above should be used to persuade politicians, the media, health professionals, key opinion leaders and the general community that this is a vital step in the fight against tobacco use.

Remember that taxing tobacco is the single most effective policy tool that can be used to reduce smoking and improve the health of the people.

3 Establishing Dedicated Taxes

3.1 History

Dedicated taxes are those which are earmarked (or 'hypothecated') for special purposes. They do not become part of general consolidated revenue and are applied to a dedicated or specific purpose.

Some of the earliest developments in this area occurred in states in Australia. For example, in Western Australia in 1983, increases in tobacco taxes resulted in a considerable injection of funds for health promotion / tobacco control activities when some US$ 1.2 million of the increase was directed to the 'Tobacco Tax Trust Fund'.[14] This was managed by the Department of Health for general health promotion programmes, with an emphasis on tobacco control.

The passing of the Tobacco Act in the Australian State of Victoria followed in 1987. This, not only led to tobacco taxes being directed to health promotion and tobacco control programmes, but also brought into being a specific organization, the Victorian Health Promotion Foundation, to administer the funding. This was the first of the new organizations set up to administer the dedicated tobacco taxes.

[14] Holman CDJ, Donovan RJ, Corti B. *Report of the evaluation of the Western Australian Health Promotion Foundation.* Perth, Health Promotion Development and Evaluation Program, Department of Public Health and Graduate School of Management, The University of Western Australia,1984:6.

While many important components of the original Victorian Bill were passed, attempts to completely ban tobacco advertising and sponsorship through the Tobacco Act were not successful. However, what was achieved was an increase in state tobacco tax, with at least part of that tax being used for health promotion programmes and research, as well as the replacement of tobacco sponsorship for those sports, arts and racing organizations which chose to relinquish their links to tobacco. [15]

This was a good result given that previous attempts to pass legislation in other Australian states had failed because the powerful sports, arts and racing lobbies had claimed that such a ban would cause hardship. Their vehement opposition to the proposed legislation meant that new and creative solutions were needed. The Victorian outcome produced, not only a win/win situation for public health groups, as well as sports, arts and racing bodies, but also set a precedent for other states and countries to model.

It was not long before a number of other Australian states followed the Victorian example by dedicating a percentage of tobacco tax for heath promotion/tobacco control activities. These were South Australia in 1988, the Australian Capital Territory in 1989, and Western Australia in 1990. The three were successful in achieving bans on tobacco advertising and sponsorship, although there were exemptions in the early days for events of national or international significance. All four of the states established new organizations, health promotion foundations, to administer the funds.

In other parts of the world there were also moves to use tobacco taxes in this way. In 1988, Californian voters approved a 25 cents per package increase on cigarette tax, a quarter of which was earmarked for anti-smoking education and tobacco-related research.[16]

The last decade has seen a number of other states and countries establish funds for health promotion /tobacco control through dedicated taxes. However, not all of these have been linked to the banning of tobacco advertising and sponsorship as they were in Australia. Examples of some countries and states which have introduced dedicated tobacco taxes for health promotion / tobacco control are listed in Appendix A.

The methods and organizational structures established to manage and administer the funds have also varied from country to country. Some countries have also used different funding bases for their health promotion activities, such as alcohol taxes and health insurance funds.

[15] Winstanley M. *Overview of the lobbying for the Victorian Tobacco Act (1987).* Melbourne, Victorian Smoking and Health Program (Quit),1993:28.

[16] Bal DG *et al.* Reducing tobacco consumption in California. Development of a statewide anti-tobacco use campaign. *Journal of the American Medical Association*, 1990, 264:1570-1574.

3.2 Processes involved in getting started

There are generally a number of stages involved in establishing dedicated taxes for tobacco control or health promotion activities, as well as developing an appropriate organizational model to allocate funds. As most states and countries experience budget constraints, there may be initial resistance to any approach to have funding quarantined from current tax revenue for specific purposes. A more positive outcome may result from first seeking an increase in tobacco tax and then making a case for part of that increase being earmarked for specific programmes. Powerful arguments can be mounted in support of using a portion of tobacco tax to address the health and social issues stemming from the use of this product.

Whether the two stages described above should occur simultaneously, or the increase in tax should be achieved prior to the case being made for funding for health promotion, is a matter for debate. In some places, like the State of Victoria, which has been successful in achieving these outcomes, negotiations took place at the same time. In others, like Thailand, two separate negotiations occurred, one to have the tax raised and the second to have part of it dedicated for health promotion initiatives which would be administered by an organization set up specifically for that purpose.

Persuading governments

It is noteworthy that governments, ministries of finance in particular, are generally not enthusiastic about earmarking taxes for specific purposes. They claim that this has the potential to distort government spending by reducing government control and its free ability to make decisions. Furthermore, it may be argued that dedicating or committing taxes for specific purposes may not allow for changing social environments and changing government priorities.

The idea of introducing funding mechanisms or agencies which control the funds, and which may operate independently of government, may also not be well received initially. It is essential, therefore, to convince those holding the purse strings that such measures are vital to provide for medium- to long-term planning and implementation of programmes which will ultimately have a positive effect on the health of the community.

Persuading governments to take this step is both a complex and challenging task, requiring much preparation and planning. In Malaysia, where relevant legislation is about to be introduced, and Thailand, which legislated in 2001, the process took around 10 years of hard work before success was achieved.

3.3 Why dedicate part or all of a tobacco tax for health promotion/ tobacco control programmes?

The establishment of new or increased levels of tobacco taxes provides an excellent opportunity to make a case for all or part of the funds being used for health promotion/ tobacco control programmes. When putting forward such a case, it is vital that the arguments are clearly articulated and explained, particularly to decision-makers.

However, it is acknowledged that such arguments are more complicated in countries where governments have a major ownership stake in the tobacco industry. Having said this, the tobacco industry is being increasingly litigated by those affected by the harmful aspects of tobacco. There may be, therefore, a stronger case for those governments directing funding towards activities that would reduce tobacco use, as one way of limiting the future liability of the government in this regard. This, however, has yet to be tested in a legal sense.

Those spearheading a campaign to raise dedicated taxes for health promotion purposes must be well informed and able to present the following arguments in a logical and convincing manner.

Direct health and other benefits of tax increases

While historically governments have tended to be reluctant to support the introduction of dedicated taxes, they do, of necessity, need to collect taxes and, from time to time, increase the percentage gathered from different commodities.

Establishing tobacco taxes can raise funds for a range of government programmes, not only health. The 15% increase in tobacco tax introduced in Western Australia in 1991 saw some 10% of the additional funds generated (US$ 6.6 million) being allocated for health promotion activities, while an additional US$ 60 million was retained in consolidated revenue for other government programmes and works. Similarly, in the State of Victoria in 1988, the original submission to increase tobacco taxes earned the Government in that state some US$ 60 million in the first year, after the allocation of US$ 15 million for health promotion programmes.[17]

In Thailand, where tobacco tax was incrementally increased from 55% to 71.5% as one way of discouraging smokers, an additional US$ 1 billion has been raised for the Government since 1993. This has contributed to reduced smoking prevalence and hence smoking-related health expenditures.[18]

When governments see that there may be financial gains, which may be applied across a range of portfolios, they tend to be more open to increasing tobacco taxes.

[17] Winstanley M. *Op cit* .Ref 16.

Many benefits may also be achieved in terms of health. The raising of taxes, which leads to price-induced decreases in cigarette smoking, translates directly into health benefits. It is estimated that one-third of people who quit because of a price increase will enjoy a significant increase in years of life.[19]

Measures which encourage smokers to quit should also be regarded as excellent investments in reducing future health care expenditure. For example, it has been estimated that, within two years of quitting, there is an effective reduction in deaths and hospitalizations, even in those with very serious cardiovascular problems.[20] Any measures which result in smokers quitting and thus reducing health care costs will be attractive to governments. They must be pursued vigorously and the potential impact of tax increases to assist in this should be exploited wherever possible.

Countering the tobacco industry

The tobacco industry spends hundreds of millions of dollars annually on research, marketing, advertising, promotion and sponsorship in order to encourage more people to smoke and to retain those who are already addicted to tobacco. It is just not possible for governments to counter the efforts of the tobacco industry because they cannot match the funds expended by it.

One creative way to raise funds is to link the funding for tobacco control to a percentage of the tax on the income stream from tobacco, dedicating or earmarking the tax for health promotion/tobacco control programmes.

A fair return to smokers

Smokers, the vast majority of whom would like to quit, contribute huge amounts to governments by way of tobacco tax. In 2001, Australian smokers contributed approximately US$ 2.76 billion per annum in government taxes on tobacco products.[21] Barely half of 1% of that amount was devoted to anti-smoking education, or around US$ 15 million per annum in combined Federal and state jurisdictions.[22] It is estimated that, while more than 90% of smokers wish to quit, between 75% and 90% will fail even very serious attempts to stop.[23] It seems fair and desirable, therefore, that a significant proportion of the tax smokers pay should be used to help them to stop smoking and also to prevent young people from starting.

---

[18] Vatessatokit P. Thai tobacco control: Development through strategic alliances. *Development Bulletin*, 2001, 54:63.

[19] Warner K. *Taxes, smuggling and duty-free*. Presentation at the INB5 meeting, Geneva, 2002.

[20] Suskin *et al*. Relationship of current and past smoking to mortality and morbidity in patients with left ventricular dysfunction. *Journal of the American College of Cardiology*, 2001, 37:1677-1682.

[21] Australian Bureau of Statistics. *Monthly tobacco excise receipts*. Canberra, Australian Bureau of Statistics, 2001.

[22] Tan N, Wakefield M, Freeman J. Changes associated with the National Tobacco Campaign. Results of the second follow up survey. In: *Australia's National Tobacco Campaign. Evaluation report volume two*. Canberra: Commonwealth Department of Health and Aged Care, 2000:21-75.

[23] *Tobacco control: a blue chip investment in public health*. Victoria, Victoria Health Centre for Tobacco Control, 2001:30.

Ability to fund a range of health-related initiatives

Such health-related initiatives may include:

- general health promotion programmes addressing such issues as injury prevention, sun protection, healthy eating, safe alcohol use and safe sex, etc.;
- tobacco control programmes, including media campaigns, advocacy, educational initiatives for young people and legislative reform;
- public health/ health promotion and tobacco-related research;
- replacement of tobacco advertising and sponsorship programmes; and/or
- telephone counselling, stop-smoking programmes and other services for smokers.

Secure funding for health promotion

The reality is that, in the budget process, the prevention and promotion areas tend to miss out because of urgent and compelling claims from the hospital and treatment services side of the health industry. However, with dedicated taxes, the income stream is separate from the main health budget, and so those dedicated taxes are more likely to remain untouched, even in a recession when there may be 'across-the-board' budget cuts.

A long-term investment

The community gains enormously by using dedicated taxes. Whether used for tobacco control or general health promotion programmes, for health promotion research, or to replace tobacco advertising and sponsorship of sport, arts and racing events, children, adults and the elderly will all benefit through exposure to such initiatives.

A means to replace tobacco advertising and sponsorship

Norway and Finland were among the first countries in the world to adopt a comprehensive ban on tobacco promotion. Relevant legislation was introduced in Norway in 1975 and in Finland in 1978. Following the bans, with the exception of internationally televised tobacco-sponsored events and advertising in international press, very little incidental advertising was evident in those countries. Rimpela and colleagues report that, in the five years following the introduction of the legislation, there was a marked decrease in the prevalence of smoking among both boys and girls, although subsequently the decline was less consistent and pronounced.[24]

[24] Rimpela *et al.* The effects of tobacco sales promotion on initiation of smoking. *Scandinavian Journal of Social Medicine, Supplement*, 1993, 49:5-23.

It is widely acknowledged that tobacco advertising and sponsorship, combined with tobacco promotion, are powerful risk factors, which are open to intervention, and their control should form part of a comprehensive approach to prevention.[25] Funds from tobacco taxes have been successfully used, particularly in Australia, to break the nexus between tobacco and sport by replacing tobacco sponsorship funds. Such funds have been used to compensate sponsored groups and organizations for specific periods to reduce financial hardship as they move away from tobacco support.

Critics of such measures will defend the rights of the tobacco and advertising industries to promote tobacco, which is a legal product. An appropriate response is to point out that the product in question, tobacco, although sold legally, is one that kills, even when used as the manufacturer intends.

A lasting funding source, despite change

Progressive tax increases have resulted in some potential setbacks in Australia, but these have generally been overcome as governments have recognized the value of the health promotion activities to which they are applied. In the states of Western Australia and Victoria, after particularly large tax increases in the early 1990s, the governments of each state capped the amounts hypothecated from tobacco tax and administered by the health promotion foundations. In Victoria, this resulted in a one-off 25% reduction in the earmarked budget. However, following the fixing of earmarked amounts, the budgets of these organizations are now subject to annual review, with indexation awarded at around the level of yearly cost-of-living increases. This means that both foundations continue to receive and distribute significant funding for health promotion activities in their respective states.

Another change which had the potential to dismantle the dedicated tax system also occurred in Australia. In 1997, the High Court of Australia ruled that it was unconstitutional for states to collect tobacco, alcohol and petrol taxes. This was deemed the right of the Commonwealth Government, which would then forward the collected taxes to the states. At that time, Australia had four health promotion foundations in four different states, each of which were being funded through a percentage of the state tobacco franchise fees. Technically the decision of the High Court of Australia removed the entire financial resources of those organizations. However, the outcome was that the four state governments continued to support the organizations at the same level as before the High Court decision, using moneys allocated directly from Federal consolidated revenue. This change had no material impact on the funding for the foundations or their ability to continue with their health promotion activities.

[25] Reid *et al.* Choosing the most effective health promotion options for reducing a nation's smoking prevalence. *Tobacco control*, 1992, 1:185-197.

In South Australia where, in 1998, the Government decided to abolish the Health Promotion Foundation, the funds administered by the organization continue to be allocated to health promotion through the Departments of Human Services, Arts and Recreation and Sport. Again the funding has remained secure and the health promotion benefits have been maintained, despite the administrative changes.

3.4 Countering the critics of tobacco tax increases

Opponents of tobacco tax increases generally cite a range of arguments to support their views. These arguments, which must be countered if taxes are to be increased, are often based on myths or misconceptions. It is important to know the reality to respond appropriately if myths are raised in connection with tobacco tax increases.[26]

Lost revenue

Myth: Tobacco tax increases will result in lost revenue. If demand for cigarettes falls when prices are increased, then revenues must fall as well.

Reality: When cigarette taxes are increased, declines in demand do not exceed gains in revenue. A study of 70 countries estimates that a 10% excise tax worldwide would increase tax revenues by about 7% overall.

Job losses

Myth: If the demand for tobacco falls there will be permanent job losses in many countries.

Reality: For all but a very few countries heavily dependent on tobacco production there would be no net loss of jobs because of declining consumption. In some cases there may even be gains. This is because, if people do not buy cigarettes, they will be able to spend their money on other goods and services. The lost jobs will be replaced with new ones. Even if tax increases were introduced right away, the decline in smoking and jobs would be gradual and the economy would have time to adjust.

Promotes smuggling

Myth: Higher cigarette taxes will result in more cigarette smuggling.

Reality: Smuggling is a serious problem that requires strict, implemented regulation. However, even when smuggling occurs at high rates, tax increases bring greater revenues and reduce consumption.

[26] *Summary of curbing the epidemic. Governments and the economics of tobacco control.* Washington DC, World Bank, 1999 (Development in Practice Series).

Penalizes the poor

Myth: Poor people are penalized more by increased tobacco taxes.

Reality: Existing taxes do consume a higher share of the income of poor consumers than rich consumers. However, poor smokers are usually more responsive to price increases than rich smokers, so their consumption of cigarettes will fall more sharply following a tax increase and their relative financial burden will be correspondingly reduced. Some methods of compensation include making other taxes progressive or using some taxation revenues to subsidize cessation programmes, products or other services for the poor. Considering that people in poverty have poorer health status, a reduction in smoking may be of greater health benefit to poor people.

An unpopular action

Myth: Increasing tobacco taxes will be unpopular with the people, who do not support tax increases.

Reality: This is a myth designed to make governments feel nervous and, therefore, reluctant to change. Interestingly, while increasing taxes is generally unpopular with the community, it becomes a popular move if tied to funding tobacco control or health promotion programmes.

Surveys carried out in Victoria, Western Australia and Thailand, prior to the introduction of tobacco legislation to raise tobacco taxes in those jurisdictions, confirm this view. For example, in Victoria a public opinion poll found that, while only 47% of people approved of an increase in tobacco tax, that number rose to 84% when part of the tax was to be used for such programmes as health education, medical research and funding for sport and the arts.[27] That result was replicated in Thailand, where 80% of those non-smokers surveyed and 65 % of smokers supported the tax increase when a proportion of the funds was to be directed to health promotion programmes.[28]

It is important to measure public opinion. In these examples, polls have been used to dispel the myth that tax increases are always unpopular, a myth which has the potential to obstruct change.

3.5 The campaign to dedicate taxes

The term 'campaign' is often used to describe the processes and strategies required to make a case for dedicated taxes for health promotion. A campaign is defined as an organized series of operations, which is exactly what is required to achieve success.

[27] Hill D. Public opinion on tobacco advertising, sports sponsorships and taxation prior to the Victorian Tobacco Act, 1987. *Community Health Studies*, 1988, XII, 3: 282-288.
[28] Ritthiphakdee Bung-on. *Op cit.* Ref 8.

Those states and countries that have increased tobacco tax for health promotion/ tobacco control initiatives and created appropriate funding mechanisms for their distribution have identified a number of key strategies. Interestingly, those that are listed below have been generally utilized in both developing and developed countries.

3.5.1 Key campaign strategies

Identify a campaign leader

The campaign leader should be someone who can spearhead and coordinate the push for increased/ dedicated taxes. Ideally the leader will be someone who is very knowledgeable about health matters and is well respected in the community, particularly by politicians. Preferably the leader will be without specific political affiliations, an articulate speaker and a good media performer. He or she should have extensive community networks and be able to work as part of a team as well as build a wide coalition of supporters. Such individuals may come from a range of settings including health departments, nongovernmental organizations (NGOs) and hospitals.

Organize a coalition of supporters

The coalition will collectively and actively participate in the campaign to increase and/or dedicate taxes. Those involved will be able to access further help from their own networks. It is important that the members of the coalition, or their organizations, be assigned roles which use their expertise and skills so that they take ownership of the campaign.

The coalition will generally be spearheaded by representatives from public health, including professional associations, academics and NGOs. Switzerland has recently been advocating for tobacco tax to be dedicated for health promotion. Their coalition includes the Tobacco Prevention Association, the Swiss Institute for Prevention of Alcohol and Drugs Problems, the Swiss Lung Association, the Swiss Cancer Association, Health Promotion Switzerland, the Swiss Society for Public Health, the Technical Agency for Health Policy and the Swiss Federal Office for Public Health.

Other areas that may be represented include:

- the community;
- medicine;
- the arts;
- education;
- relevant government departments;
- ministerial staff;

- the media;
- sport; or
- churches.

Establish an evidence base

It is vital to undertake research in order to convince decision-makers that raising taxes will be economically cost-effective as well as having positive health benefits. The evidence may cover such areas as numbers of smokers and the potential impact of the tax on consumption, particularly in relation to children. As has already been stated, research carried out in Thailand prior to taxes being raised there estimated that a tobacco tax increase of 6% would prevent some 200 000 young people from starting to smoke.[29] This sent a very powerful message to the Thai decision-makers.

Assess public opinion

Surveys will determine the level of community support for the dedicated tax. Politicians are more likely to take actions that are popular with their constituents. Market research will also provide data with which to counter the tobacco industry if scare tactics are introduced, such as claiming that the community opposes tobacco tax increases.

Plan an extensive public awareness campaign

Placing the subject on the community agenda and educating people about the issues are important steps. It is important to concentrate on the heath benefits of the proposed changes and the health of the community, particularly that of children.

A public awareness campaign does not have to be costly to succeed. One of the morning papers in Victoria, 'The Age', was enlisted as a strong supporter of the campaign to increase taxes and it published regular articles, editorials and letters. Press and radio interviews, radio talk-back shows and letters to the editor are all no-cost ways of getting the message across during the campaign period.[30]

In Australia, where the banning of tobacco advertising and sponsorship was linked to the proposed tax increases, press advertising was used in a limited way to alert the public to the issues. For example, in Western Australia a press advertisement featured around 30 high profile people, representing different sports, acknowledging that sport would be much better off without tobacco sponsorship. There were also a number of staged publicity events. In Victoria, for example, several prominent sporting identities signed a petition in the city square in support of the legislation. The event attracted many onlookers and obtained wide media coverage.[31]

[29] Ritthiphakdee Bung-on. *Op cit.* Ref 8.
[30] Winstanley M. *Op cit.* Ref 16:14,15.
[31] *Ibid*: 22.

Prepare draft legislation

While the government of the day will draft the final legislation, it will be useful to have a clear concept towards which to work. Such draft legislation is a useful tool for lobbying and it will help to clarify what is being proposed. The legislation will ideally link the dedicated tax to a percentage of tobacco taxation. The exact mechanism for collecting the levy that might take the form of an excise duty, a tobacco franchise fee or other mechanism, and will depend upon the administrative and legislative structures in place for collecting tobacco tax.

Appendix A includes a list of some relevant legislation which may be used as examples, and the Pan American Health Organization (PAHO) has recently produced a useful document, with templates for tobacco control legislation, that includes a section on advertising and promotion.[32]

3.5.2 Successful lobbying and advocacy for change

A successful campaign will require a strategic approach to political lobbying and advocacy. The Victorian experience, which used a three-stage approach to lobbying, has been well documented.[33] [34]

The **first phase** involves convincing the Cabinet, or the equivalent of the parliamentary executive, that it should act. It is important that the Minister for Health is supportive from the outset and the Prime Minister or Premier is also a crucial ally. Another key individual in Cabinet is the Treasurer (or Minister of Finance), who will be required to support the taxation increase and hypothecation aspects of the Bill when it goes forward.

Relevant parliamentary committees also need to be persuaded and these may include the committees that consider matters concerned with government finances and health policy. It is also useful to have support from the Minister who controls the legislative agenda in Parliament. Other key Cabinet personnel may be identified as potential supporters, such as a former Minister for Health, a Minister for Sport or even a parliamentarian who is a reformed smoker. One of the tasks of the coalition is to identify key potential supporters and work on them.

After the proposed legislation has received Cabinet support the **second phase** of lobbying involves gaining the support of the Parliamentary Opposition. Ideally, legislation of this type would have bipartisan support. If that is achieved, the legislation will pass smoothly through the parliamentary process, leading to smooth implementation of the new structures. In the likely event of there not being unanimous support from the Opposition, it is certainly worthwhile trying to win support of at least some key Opposition members. Important individuals include the Opposition Spokesperson for Health and the Opposition Leader.

[32] *Developing legislation for tobacco control. Template and guidelines*. Washington DC, Pan American Health Organization, June 2003.

[33] Winstanley M. *Op cit.* Ref 16:11-14.

[34] Gray N. Public health, preventive medicine, politics and the law. Australian Cancer Society,*Cancer Forum*, 12,1:5-8.

In Victoria, these phases one and two overlapped in their timing. They were also backed up by carefully planned publicity activities designed to raise the issue high on the public agenda and to increase political interest and resolve.

The **third phase** has been described as 'the public battle'.[35] This took place in Victoria when the Government made public its intention to pursue the piece of legislation, the Tobacco Control Bill. It is at this stage that the health lobby must be very active in countering opposition from the tobacco industry, their allies and other vested interests likely to make huge efforts to stop the progress of the Bill by pressuring politicians into rejecting it. Parliamentary lobbying must focus on reinforcing and strengthening government resolve at this crucial stage. Lobbying must counter the often underhand tactics of the tobacco industry which, at this stage in Australia, publicly opposed the proposed legislation with a media campaign based on misinformation and fear.

Letter-writing campaign

A powerful lobbying strategy is to make contact with parliamentarians through an organized letter-writing campaign as well as making personal visits. This will dispel the line generally put forward by the tobacco industry that tobacco legislative changes are merely the wish of a minority group or anti-tobacco zealots.

Suitable mailing lists should be planned and compiled using the contacts and networks of coalition personnel. Potential letter writers should be provided with short briefing notes about the health issues, reasons for the proposed legislation and an outline of what the legislation should cover. The writer should be asked to use his/ her own background and expertise to frame a letter that will reflect particular individual concerns or those of the organization represented. The letters should be sent to all members of Parliament as well as other community leaders and decision-makers.

In Victoria, it is estimated that well in excess of 150 000 letters were sent within a month. The Opposition Spokesperson for Health estimated he had received more that 10 000 letters on the issue from both sides and many parliamentarians reported that they had never before received so many communications on a single issue.

A second strategy is to ask coalition members to visit their own parliamentary representatives to discuss the matter.[36]

A number of lessons have been learned from the unsuccessful Western Australia attempts to introduce legislation in the early 1980s. These may be summarized as follows:

- As it is not possible to match the tobacco industry's rate of expenditure, it is unwise to try to compete in terms of bought advertising and publicity.

[35] Winstanley M. *Op cit.* Ref 16 :11.
[36] *Ibid*: 16.

- The health lobby must set the agenda for debate and that agenda should focus on the health of adults and children. The tobacco industry may raise arguments about the unpopularity of raising tobacco taxes, on the lack of impact of advertising and sponsorship on consumption and that the proposed measures take away the freedom of choice of individuals. It is important not to buy into these arguments or other diversionary issues that may be raised.
- If the banning of advertising and sponsorship is part of the plan, it is important to publicize early and widely that alternative replacement funds will be available so that no individual or group will suffer immediate hardship. This may limit anxiety and concern among those who may be affected, and will also limit potentially damaging publicity.
- It is recommended that the length of the period for public debate be kept to a minimum. The longer the time, the more opportunity the tobacco industry has to use its massive resources to sway public opinion in its favour.

3.6 Key steps to success

Based on the experience of a number of states and countries where dedicated taxes have been installed, a number of key steps to success have been identified. These may be summarized as follows.

- Before beginning, ensure there is a positive political climate. TIMING IS VITAL.
- Develop a well planned campaign that has strong leadership and a wide range of supporters.
- Be clear about how the dedicated tobacco tax is to be used. Also have strong views about the funding mechanisms and administrative structures which would be ideal for the management and allocation of the funds. Prepare draft legislation. Strive towards the ideal models, but be prepared to compromise if this is not entirely attainable.
- Undertake thorough research to support the case for dedicated tax, concentrating on the health outcomes which will result.
- Strive for some degree of bipartisan support. This will make the passage of the legislation less difficult and will also facilitate the implementation of the new structures once the legislation is proclaimed. It should also help to ensure the continuation of a tobacco tax should a change of government occur and be followed by lobbying of the new government by the tobacco industry.
- Work within a short time-frame so that opposition does not have time to gather momentum.
- Ensure that expert information is readily available and that all the facts are correct.
- Use a professional approach in all activities, including lobbying, letter writing, publicity and public relations.

- Use market research to assess community support for the proposed changes; this may be used as a lever for change.
- Before drafting legislation, examine that of other jurisdictions. Talk to others about the positive aspects and pitfalls of their legislation and learn from their experience.
- Be prepared for opposition from the tobacco industry, which will need to be countered efficiently and effectively to ensure success.
- Set attainable goals. If the legislation is not perfect, be prepared to compromise so long as some benefits are gained. It may be possible to amend and strengthen the legislation at a later date.
- Always maintain the high moral ground. Increasing tobacco tax and dedicating part or all of it to health promotion/ tobacco control is about improving health, the health of children and adults.

Gray concludes his comments with the statement that "the introduction Victorian Tobacco Act required a ridiculous amount of work by an extraordinarily large number of people to introduce a straightforward piece of legislation which conforms to public health policy."[37]

However, it is well worth the effort. Remember that tobacco smoking is the single major preventable cause of death and disease in the world today. Currently tobacco kills one in ten adults worldwide. By 2030, it is estimated that proportion will be one in six, amounting to 10 million people per year.[38] Firm and speedy action is necessary.

[37] Gray. *Op cit.* Ref 35:8.
[38] World Bank. *Op cit.* Ref 5:1.

4 Organizational Structures for Administering Funding

4.1 Introduction

New funding for health promotion/tobacco control activities requires new organizational structures to administer the funds. While earlier sections of this report have focused on tobacco tax as a dedicated source of funding, it should be noted that the past decade has seen a number of countries and states utilizing different financial sources in order to fund new health promotion organizations and programmes. Table 1 provides examples of different sources of funds and the purposes for which they are used.

Table 1: Examples of sources and uses of funds

Country	Organization	Legislation	Source of funds	Amount generated P/A	Population	Purpose
Austria	Austrian Health Promotion, began 1998 www.gesundesleben.at Model 1	Fund Healthy Austria Health Promotion Act	Consolidated revenue	US$ 7.9 million	8 million	To fund activities which will maintain, promote and improve the health of the Austrian population.
Hungary	Health 21 Hungarian Foundation Model 1	Nongovernmental organization – A public service corporation	World Health Organization World Bank & others			Funds are used to develop a range of effective interventions in health promotion.
New Zealand	Health Sponsorship Council www.healthsponsorship.co.nz Model 3	The Smokefree Environments Act 1990 http://www.legislation.gov.nz/	Consolidated revenue	US$ 4.5 million	4 million	Initially to buy out of tobacco sponsorship, currently funds are used for tobacco control, sun safety and injury prevention.
Switzerland	Health Promotion Switzerland www.gesundheitsfoerderung.ch Model 1	Article 19 of the Law on Sickness Insurance 1996	Medical insurance companies which contribute SF 2.40 per annum for every insured person.	US$ 12 million	7 million	Focus on empowerment, cooperation, health promotion policy, projects of Swiss cantons and international affairs.
New Zealand	Alcohol Advisory Council of New Zealand www.alcohol.org.nz	Alcohol Advisory Council Act 1976 http://www.legislation.gov.nz/	A levy on alcohol produced or imported for sale within New Zealand	US$ 8 million	4 million	Reduce alcohol-related harm, mainly through education and research.

Whatever the source of the funds, a major decision will be the type of organization which will be established to administer them. In discussing the Thai approach, Moodie[39] stresses that it is critically important for the development and sustainability of a country's health promotion efforts that an organizational structure be developed as a foundation for them. Such a structure serves as a focus for health promotion development and coordination and also supports the building of health promotion capacity.

Before describing the kinds of structures which may be considered, it is important to review the steps which should be undertaken prior to the establishment of the health promotion organization.

These include:

- making a case for an appropriate organizational structure, after considering the options;
- developing a clearly formulated and strong legislative framework; and
- formulating principles of good governance.

4.2 Making a case for an appropriate organizational structure

The injection of significant sums of new money for health promotion/tobacco programmes brings its own challenges as well as opportunities to make a real difference to the health of the community. Ideally it will result in the establishment of a new separate organization or entity with a degree of flexibility and independence. Whatever the operational model selected, the new entity will be required to perform a number of tasks and roles. These will depend on the legislative parameters that have been set, but may include:

- funding of innovative pilot health promotion programmes, with the ability to maintain long-term support for those projects which are successful and produce excellent health promotion outcomes;
- health promotion research, which may be commissioned or initiated by researchers and funded by the organization;
- replacement of tobacco sponsorship and advertising;
- health promotion initiatives in a range of settings, such as sport, the arts, racing, education or workplaces;
- development of funded services, like telephone counselling, for smokers wishing to quit;

---

[39] Moodie R *et al*. Health promotion in South- East Asia:, Indonesia, DPR Korea, Thailand, the Maldives and Myanmar. *Health Promotion International*, 2000, Vol 15, 3: 249- 257.

- facilitation of health promotion alliances through a range of settings and organizations;
- evaluation and monitoring of health promotion outcomes of funded projects and research;
- dissemination of health promotion knowledge;
- setting of the agenda for the health promotion debate;
- advocacy for, and development of health promotion policy;
- building of the capacity of the health promotion workforce, as well as the community and organizations; and
- evaluation of the impact of projects funded, as well as the work of the organization itself.

Establishing an appropriate organizational model that is able to undertake most or all of the above roles, depending on legislative requirements, is crucial to the success of the initiative. There will, no doubt, be a number of interested parties wishing to promote a certain model or mechanism for managing and disbursing the funds. Furthermore, there may be organizations or departments already established and willing to take on the role. However, for a number of reasons, this should generally be discouraged.

4.2.1 Lobbying and advocacy

Just as coordination and planning are required in order to raise tobacco taxes and have them dedicated for health promotion/tobacco control activities, these skills are again needed to ensure that the appropriate funding mechanism is established. The same group which prepared and lobbied to establish the dedicated tax may also take on this task. The issue of organizational structure may be proactively addressed at the same time as the other previously described activities are undertaken.

It has been suggested that the lobby group should be formed as a response to the demands of health groups, including NGOs working in particular areas.[40] If no such pressure exists, the first task of the lobby group will be to market its ideas and concepts to others to garner enough support to influence government and bureaucracy.

Once the group is established it will be necessary to conceptualize the ideal outcome towards which to strive, recognizing that there may need to be changes and compromises along the way.

---

[40] *Ibid*: 249.

Important considerations for the lobby group

Those making a case for establishing new mechanisms for funding should consider the following:

- Before doing anything, it is vital to determine whether there is any political support for such an initiative. If there is seemingly no backing, it is wise not to progress until there is at least some interest at government level. Ideally the Health Minister plus the Finance Minister would be supportive. If this is not forthcoming, the first task is to work towards this outcome. In Thailand, the Minister of Finance was an early supporter of the concept, which was seen as complementing the national Fiscal and Financial Master Plan for Social Development.
- The ability to address health issues through prevention and health promotion must always be cited as the major reason for seeking new funding mechanisms. Emphasis should centre on the health and other benefits which will follow for the population.
- The case should be based on evidence, which will require the gathering of baseline data highlighting population health status and trends. For example, if tobacco control is to be the major focus of the new body, data on prevalence and the uptake rate among children are essential.
- The establishment of a new and separate entity with a degree of flexibility and independence is desirable. This kind of structure will be required to be able to undertake all of the tasks described above in a timely manner, without bureaucratic impediments.
- The entity and its funding must be supported by legislation to ensure political and administrative barriers to changing either the organization or its funding source once the legislation is established.
- Whatever the model, it will include transparent and open financial accounting arrangements, which must be independently audited. The organization will have significant funding for health promotion/ tobacco control. The outcomes of the programmes, as well as the management of the funds, will be subject to much scrutiny, particularly by those groups that may have opposed the establishment of the dedicated taxes. It is therefore important to demonstrate that these funds are well managed and accounted for.
- The new public health approaches, involving the community, the environment and different settings, require new kinds of infrastructures to be established. They rely on true partnerships being formed, as well as a commitment to decentralization of health programmes. The structure selected must enable genuine community initiatives to be generated, thus leading to the empowerment of people.
- It may be prudent to propose that the operations of the funding organization be reviewed after a period of time to assess its effectiveness in relation to its objectives.

Before drafting legislation, it is important to consider the kind of organizational structure which will best suit or which may be most acceptable to the country or state This will influence the legislative content. Reviewing relevant legislation from other jurisdictions is a useful first step towards preparing legislation and will ensure the establishment of an efficient, effective and accountable funding structure.

4.2.2 Legislative requirements

The importance of having a strong legislative framework to safeguard the funds has been stressed already. It is equally important that the legislation addresses the purposes for which the funds are to be used and the kinds of organizational structures which will be put in place to administer those funds.

A number of different models or mechanisms have already been established, and these will be described in detail below. The content of the legislation will clearly reflect the kind of organizational structure to be introduced and the specifics will differ greatly depending on the mechanism selected. However, an examination of some of the available statutes reveals some common areas in relation to the funding mechanisms which have been established. These include:

- The overall purposes of the Act, which are generally broad statements indicating what the Act is intended to achieve. For example, the purpose of the legislation may be to actively discourage tobacco smoking and to promote good health and prevent illness.
- A description of the organization's legal status, eg. body corporate.
- A statement about the organization's relationship with the relevant minister and/or relevant government department. This covers reporting requirements, and whether ministerial directions may be given.
- Clearly defined objectives for the organization. These will spell out what the organization is required to do and may cover such areas as funding tobacco sponsorship replacement, providing grants to organizations engaged in health promotion programmes and/or health promotion research, or other activities which support the purposes of the Act.
- The size and method of appointment of the governing body. If relevant, this may expand to include terms of appointment and remuneration allowances, as well as refer to the decision-making processes to be employed.
- Legislation will refer to the powers of the organization, based on the objectives which have been set. These tend to clarify and expand upon the tasks which will be undertaken by the organization.

- The source and level of funding for the organization will generally be included. If the source of funds is tobacco tax, the amount, preferably a percentage of the wholesale sales tax or other tax amount, should be included. In some cases the amount of funding may be specified in other legislation. Ideally the funding level and source will be specified in legislation and will not be the subject of any discretionary policy which may lead to reduced amounts during tight budgetary periods. There may also be reference to other sources of funds that the organization may be permitted to accept or earn (eg. donations, grants or other government appropriations, as well as funds which may result from production or marketing activities). Reference to the method and frequency of payment of funds to the organization is important. This may cover how the funds are to be paid, into which account they are to be placed and the treatment of interest accruing.
- The legislation may contain some constraints. There may be time limits set in relation to the disbursement of the funds or a stipulation that a minimum percentage of the funds must be allocated to certain areas, such as health promotion research or health promotion through sport. There may also be activities which the fund will not support, such as clinical research.
- A requirement may also be included for the operations of the funding organization to be reviewed after a period of time to assess its effectiveness in relation to its objectives.

Before drafting legislation it is important to consider the kind of organizational structure which will best suit, or be most acceptable to, the country or state involved. Reviewing funding mechanisms which have been used in other jurisdictions is a useful first step towards developing concepts and models which will ultimately lead to the establishment of an efficient, effective and accountable funding structure.

4.2.3 Appointing a governing body

One of the most crucial decisions concerns the appointment of a governing body to oversee the new entity responsible for administering the funds. Important considerations include the selection method for members, the interests that they will represent, and whether parliamentarians will be eligible for membership. Appointments of governing board members may be carried out using a range of methods and formulae. In most cases, appointments are made by ministers, generally ministers of health. However, where ministerial appointments are made without any particular criteria having been established, there is the potential for political influence and bias.

The Thai Board is chaired by the Prime Minister and the Vice-Chair is the Minister for Health. Estonia also has high profile government ministers on the governing body, while the Victorian Health Promotion Foundation (Vic Health) has parliamentarians representing the three major political parties on the board to avoid political bias. The Western Australian Health Promotion Foundation (Healthway), on the other hand, does not include parliamentary representatives on its Board. Indeed the Western Australian legislation goes to great lengths to remove Healthway from any possibility of political interference, or the perception of it, by excluding Members of Parliament from being associated with any payments made by the organization, or their photographs being included in any of the organization's publications.

Some boards comprise nominees of particular organizations, covering the spectrum of activities in which the organization is involved. In some cases, like Healthway, the relevant organizations are named in the enabling legislation. Research, health promotion, sport, arts and regional interests may all be included using this model of nomination. Others have criteria which cover the relevant skills and expertise required for the efficient and effective functioning of the organization. These may include business, law, media and public relations, as well as the more traditional professional backgrounds.

In Estonia, the highest body of the Health Insurance Fund has, in roughly equal numbers, government representation, consumers representing the interests of insured persons, and nominees of employers. The Austrian Health Promotion Foundation, on the other hand, has a board of 13 members, about half of whom are government appointees. The remainder are nominees of such organizations as the Association of Austrian Cities, Association of Austrian Municipalities, Austrian Medical Association, Austrian Pharmacists' Association and the Association of Austrian Private Insurance Companies.

Health Promotion Switzerland has a board of 17 members, elected by the Swiss Federal Department of Home Affairs, and has federal as well as canton (local government) representation. The board also has the support of a nine-member advisory committee, selected on the basis of individual knowledge and skills.

However the governing body is appointed and structured, it should be able to operate equitably, independently and without fear or favour. Its general selection and operational criteria should be included in the legislation so that there are barriers to change for political or other reasons. Sound governance procedures and protocols will further strengthen the operational environment of the board.

4.2.4 Governance

It is very important to address the issue of governance no matter what type of organizational structure is established. Corporate governance may be described as the processes, systems and standards involved in directing, controlling and adding value to an organization and its stakeholders.[41] Such processes and systems entail the setting of strategic directions, the development of organizational policies, and the establishment of expectations for management performance and the monitoring of achievements against these.

[41] Victorian Health Promotion Foundation. Governance Charter, 2003: 5.

As significant funds will be placed under the management of the organization, it is vital that a framework is established for organizational accountability and for defining boundaries between the responsibilities of boards of management, committees and paid staff. Vic Health's comprehensive Governance Charter provides an excellent model which is worthy of consideration.[42] The Charter spells out the organization's approach to a range of areas including:

- Governance practice which covers such matters as: values; the role of the Board; legislation and relationship with the Government; board focus; the role of the Chair; selection, appointments and induction of board members; care, skill and diligence requirements; board meetings; board advisory processes; delegations; and reviews of board performances.
- Corporate relationships which cover such matters as: the relationship between the Board and the chief executive office (CEO); the role of the CEO; CEO assessment; and risk management strategies, including financial, operational and personnel management.
- Strategic direction setting and monitoring, which covers such matters as: setting directions; the process for determining strategic directions; performance monitoring; evaluation and quality assurance; reporting schedule; and compliance and reporting framework.

An organization practising sound governance will publish codes of conduct and proper practice to be followed by management, staff and advisory committees, as well as those who work in organizations which receive funding for projects and sponsorships. For those who are in decision-making positions there must be a requirement to declare interests in applications or projects under consideration and it is, therefore, necessary to prepare an appropriate policy and procedures manual.

A comprehensive governance policy, developed and widely disseminated in the early stages of the new organization's establishment phase, will do much to build confidence that the organization will fulfil its statutory responsibilities while acting ethically and prudently.

4.2.5 Setting the objectives and priorities of the organization

The broad objectives of the funding body are likely to be included in the enabling legislation and, if so, there may be comparatively little flexibility, depending on how these are stated. There will, however, be opportunities to develop more specific objectives for the organization to address and it is important to identify priorities and directions for action in the early stages and to advise stakeholders of these. Lessons can be learned from the Health Promotion Commission in Estonia, which used the following criteria to establish priorities:

- burden of disease;
- cost of treatments for various diseases;

[42] *Ibid*. 2-26.

- amenability to change through health promotion strategies;
- consultation with other health agencies and stakeholders to avoid duplication; and
- consideration of the roles and responsibilities of other organizations.

Priorities may relate to specific health areas and population groups, the determinants of health behaviour, etc. They may also focus on such issues as capacity building or working in partnership with a range of organizations and in different settings. A critical step in the early establishment phase is the development of a strategic plan that clearly prioritizes key goals and strategies to address the stated objectives of the organization.

4.3 Organizational structures

There are a number of organizational structures which may be employed to administer funds for health promotion/ tobacco control. This section examines a range of such structures and highlights the advantages and disadvantages of each. There is no ideal model. Indeed, it is possible to select components of different models which may best suit the needs and environments of each country or state.

4.3.1 The health promotion foundation model (Model 1)

The newest and perhaps most innovative model is the health promotion foundation. For the purpose of this report, a health promotion foundation is defined as an independent statutory body which has, as its major purpose, the promotion of health. (The term 'health promotion foundation' in this case does not include foundations which are funded through philanthropy, like the California Wellness Foundation or the Kansas Health Promotion Foundation).

Health promotion foundations have been described as "an Australian invention designed to solve a health problem which was also a political problem".[43] They were established initially in the 1980s and early 1990s in four Australian states after tobacco sponsorship had been banned through state legislation. A levy on tobacco taxes was used to fund the 'buy-out' of tobacco sponsorships and advertising, as well as to fund a range of other health-promoting activities. Health promotion foundations were established to administer those funds.

Since then, health promotion foundations have been established in a number of countries and states. They are funded from a range of sources and not necessarily from tobacco tax. Most of the foundations are members of the International Network of Health Promotion Foundations, an organization established in 1999 to enhance the performance of existing health promotion foundations and support the establishment of new ones.[44]

[43] Daube M. Health promotion foundations in Australia. *Health Promotion Journal of Australia*, 1993, 3,1:3.
[44] International Network of Health Promotion Foundations. *Op cit* 3.

Characteristics of health promotion foundations

The International Network of Health Promotion Foundations has identified a number of characteristics as those which best describe this type of organization.[45] They include the following:

- The organization is primarily involved in funding health promotion activities.
- The organization has been established according to some form of legislation, such as an Act of Parliament.
- The legislation provides a long-term and recurrent budget for the purpose of health promotion.
- The organization is governed by an independent board that comprises stakeholder representation and is not involved in the day-to-day direction of the organization.
- The organization exercises a high level of autonomous decision-making and uses transparent and equitable allocation procedures.
- The organization is not aligned with any one political group and encourages support across the political spectrum.
- The organization promotes health by working with and across many sectors and levels of society.

Of particular relevance, and what sets the health promotion foundation model apart, is the relative independence from government and the ability to make autonomous decisions about programmes, policies and funding.

Generally, government will maintain some control, for example by making appointments to the board and approving budgets. However, the foundations usually make independent decisions about health priorities and the allocation of their funds, and then report to government on what has been achieved.

Health promotion foundations have different ways of operating. Some will plan and deliver health promotion programmes, while others use their funds to enable and empower such programmes, or they may combine both approaches. Some will commission specific research or health projects to be undertaken, while others may only deal with applications and the funding/supervision of the projects so approved, or again they may combine both approaches.

[45] The International Network of Health Promotion Foundations. *Network Policies*, 2002.

Health promotion foundations are multifaceted, with the ability to complete all the tasks and roles which have been identified in section 4.2 as those which must be accommodated within the new mechanisms for funding. **One of their strengths is that they work in partnership with government, nongovernmental and community-based organizations, enabling and empowering them to carry out health promotion programmes and initiatives.** Countries or states wishing to establish the health promotion foundation model as a mechanism for funding should be mindful of the above characteristics as they develop the organizational structure.

Examples of health promotion foundations include: The Thai Health Promotion Foundation (ThaiHealth www.thaihealth.or.th), The Victorian Health Promotion Foundation (VicHealth www.vichealth.vic.gov.au) and the Estonian Health Promotion Commission.

Advantages of the health promotion foundation model include the ability to:

- operate independently of government while supporting government priorities and directions for health promotion;
- gain support from all political parties;
- plan and implement long-term health promotion/tobacco control programmes because the funding is enshrined in legislation and, therefore, guaranteed;.
- protect health promotion programmes from cancellation or change because of political or other influences;
- more easily replace tobacco advertising and sponsorship using health promotion messages because the structure lends itself to working in a commercial environment;
- utilize its independence to advocate strongly to government in relation to health promotion policy;
- trial innovative programmes which may be risky or politically sensitive and are unlikely to be undertaken by health departments because of their potential to expose governments to criticism;
- operate openly, equitably, accountably and quickly without bureaucratic constraints; and
- work across a range of sectors including health, sport, the arts, education, transport and community development.

Disadvantages of the health promotion foundation model

There are few disadvantages to this model if it is established on the basis of sound legislation, which includes quarantined and confirmed funds and a strong governing body, without political bias. However, because the funding is guaranteed through legislation, it is not possible for the foundation's funds to be redirected to other needy areas in times of budget constraints or cutbacks and this may lead to tensions with other areas, like health departments, if their funding or programmes become threatened.

One way to counter this potential difficulty is to have close links with the health or other relevant departments, to generally follow country and state health priorities and to include appropriate representation on the foundation's advisory committees. Having appropriate government representation will also minimize the possibility of duplication, which has the potential to occur if there is more than one agency involved in health promotion.

4.3.2 The unit within a government department model (Model 2)

A health promotion arm funded through the dedicated tax may be set up within the appropriate government structure such as in a department of health, as a separate unit or a branch within the department. In this kind of arrangement, many of the roles and functions which are required of the funding body may be undertaken. There is no doubt that this model may be attractive to some governments, which may be resistant to committing large sums of money to an organization which, through its structure, is at arms length from government.

Examples of this kind of organizational structure include the Health Promotion Development Centre, which operates within the Korean Institute for Health and Social Affairs (www.kihasa.re.kr). Following an increase in tobacco tax in 2002, some 3% of the funds, around US$ 17 million, was allocated to the Centre for health promotion activities. The remainder is used for health insurance.[46]

The advantages of establishing a unit within a government department include the ability to:

- fully support and implement government public health policies, priorities and strategies because of close working relationship, integration and sound coordination with other areas within the department;
- gain direct access to government through the minister and departmental director (this has the potential to enable the Health Promotion Unit to influence policy and direction for health promotion in the state or country);
- minimize the potential for duplication of funding or effort;

[46] Nam J. *Overview of health promotion in Korea.* Presentation to the International Network of Health Promotion Foundations. Bangkok, 2002.

- access the expertise and resources of a range of other departmental units; and
- minimize the potential for tension or conflict, as health agencies are not competing for the health promotion dollar.

Disadvantages of placing a unit within a government department

- There will be direct ministerial control and this is likely to reduce its independence. Programmes and activities may be implemented because of political or other pressures, rather than because they address priority issues and populations.
- There is also the possibility that there may be political influence in relation to decisions about grants and sponsorships.
- The Unit's ability to undertake innovative and perhaps controversial programmes and activities may be limited because they may be unpalatable to the Government.
- There may be competition from within the Department of Health for resources. The debate about whether funding should be directed towards prevention rather than treatment and services is ongoing and relevant in most countries. Provided the health promotion funding is quarantined through legislation, there should be no danger of funds being redirected from the prevention to the curative side. However, if the funds are located within the Department, and there is no independent board overseeing the financial transactions, there may be the potential for ministerial directions and legislative amendments to enable the transfer of funds in times of financial pressure.
- The Unit's capacity may be limited by the bureaucratic requirements that are invariably associated with being part of a government department. Such requirements may affect the ability of the Unit to respond quickly to emerging health issues or even to provide grants or sponsorships in a timely manner. If working with sport, arts and racing groups to replace tobacco sponsorship is one of the designated roles of the Unit, this may present difficulties. Working in such an environment requires the ability to operate in a commercial milieu. It also requires employees to be prepared to work hours and in situations that are not generally required of public servants.

4.3.3 The composite model (Model 3)

This model is a hybrid or combination of the two organizational structures described above, taking elements from each. It is best understood by examining an actual example of a health promotion agency which works in this way.

This model can be found in New Zealand where there is a contract between the Health Sponsorship Council (www.healthsponsorship.co.nz) and the Ministry of Health to deliver health outcomes which are agreed in consultation with the Ministry and approved by the Minister of Health. The Ministry determines the budget and health priority areas for the Health Sponsorship Council. Funding is not, therefore, tied to tobacco taxes, although some 75% of the budget is currently applied to the area of tobacco control.

The Health Sponsorship Council has a Board of up to six Directors who are appointed by the Minister of Health. Although funding is determined through a three-year agreement, each year the Council must submit, for the Minister's approval, a budget, a strategic plan and an annual plan, all of which are endorsed before funds are committed. While having limited flexibility and independence, the Health Sponsorship Council is structured in such a way that there is autonomy in decision-making within the financial and priority issues framework which has been agreed by the Minister.

In the early 1990s, the buy-out of tobacco sponsorship was a major task of the Council. In fact this was the main reason for the Council's establishment under the Smoke-Free Environments Act 1990. However, buying out tobacco sponsorship was a transitional measure, designed to lessen the impact of introducing a ban on tobacco sponsorship, and it was always envisaged that those being sponsored would only receive assistance from the Council for a limited time while they sought other sources of sponsorship. No such obligation with respect to buying out tobacco sponsorship now exists, as this transition period has ended.

A similar example of this model currently operates in South Australia.

4.4 Key steps to success

The lobby group's role is to inform the decision-makers about the optimal funding mechanism proposed for the state or country. In doing so, the group needs to consider, not only what will work best, but also which model is likely to be accepted. While conceptualizing and planning the ideal, it may be necessary to compromise, because, whatever the model, there will be new funds delivered to health promotion.

A number of health promotion organizations were asked to highlight the key advice they would give to those commencing the process of developing new funding mechanisms for health promotion. Their comments are summarized below:

- Monitor the political climate and assess the level of support before publicly committing to the venture. There must be some level of political support or there is little chance of success.
- Establish the support of strong advocates and develop a well structured campaign.
- Map the current health status of the population, including smoking prevalence, if tobacco control is going to be a major objective. Such evidence may be used as a persuasive argument to support need. It may also serve as baseline data for future evaluation.
- Focus on health issues and the benefits which will accrue to the health of the population.
- Be prepared to invest in building health promotion capacity so that the organization has competent personnel with whom to work.

- Develop a sound legislative basis which will ensure long-term funding and security as well as confirm the major goals.
- Implement a structure which will remove the organization from political or other influences which may impact negatively on its work.
- Ensure that the governing body is appropriately representative, that its members are knowledgeable about health promotion, as well as broader societal and political issues, and that they are prepared to operate in an equitable and accountable manner.
- Plan and advocate for the ideal organizational structure. However, if necessary, be prepared to negotiate and find middle ground which will ensure that health promotion/ tobacco control in your state or country benefits.

5 Evaluating the Impact

5.1 Introduction

When members and associates of the Network of Health Promotion Foundations were asked to list the most important initial tasks that a new health promotion agency has to complete, more than one reply included the need to establish a sound framework for evaluation.[47] With so many other immediate and pressing issues to attend to, a fledgling organization may ignore implementation of an evaluation plan and important data from the early years of operation may be lost.

One way to ensure that appropriate evaluation is undertaken is to include an objective relating to evaluation within the enabling legislation. For example, the West Australian Tobacco Control Act specifies that an ongoing objective is to evaluate and report on the effectiveness of the Foundation in achieving health promotion activities.[48] If evaluation is part of the legislative mandate, it will be seen as important and will need to be adequately resourced. However, even without such a legislative requirement, there remain compelling reasons to undertake comprehensive evaluation.

- Significant funding from dedicated tobacco taxes, administered using new funding mechanisms, can be expected to attract a high level of interest and scrutiny by government, the media and the community. In some cases, such as that of the New Zealand Health Sponsorship

---

[47] *Op cit.* Ref 2.

[48] *Western Australian Tobacco Control Act 1990.* Section 22 (1) G.

Council, where funding is determined through a three-year agreement which is subject to ministerial approval of an annual operational plan and budget, it is important to be able to provide information on the impact of the funds. This will help in future negotiations for funding and also assures agencies required to monitor the use of government money (such as the Ministries of Health or Finance), that the funds are being well used and should continue. Whether or not funding is dedicated and set in legislation, there can be challenges, particularly from Ministries of Finance, to using funds for this type of purpose (despite it being in line with the policies and wishes of the government of the day).

- Through a comprehensive evaluation programme the organization will be better able to justify that it is meeting its objectives and delivering value for money.
- The concept of using dedicated tax for tobacco control and health promotion activities is a relatively new but growing trend. Those who have begun the process have an obligation to the international community to record and disseminate results so that the model may develop internationally from a sound base of scientific knowledge.
- Experimental studies that investigate the effectiveness of sponsorship and other social marketing strategies can be mounted as part of an evaluation programme with cooperation from grant recipients. Such studies have the potential to guide and inform, leading to the refinement of strategies, particularly related to the more innovative aspects of health promotion.
- Evaluation is an essential component of every health promotion project funded, as a matter of good practice, and should be required to be undertaken by each grant recipient.

The development of a framework for evaluation is one of the most important and complex tasks to be undertaken, and it is important to take a practical approach which will produce a meaningful and realistic outcome.

5.2 A realistic approach to evaluation

Policy-makers and others tend to have high expectations of what may be achieved by new funding organizations in the short or even medium term. There may be expectations that the organization will demonstrate a contribution to economic development, as well as measurable health improvements, in a relatively short time. Such expectations are unlikely to be realized and may be damaging if not corrected. There are a number of factors which affect an evaluation programme.

5.2.1 Not working in isolation

In the majority of states and countries, the new health agency will not work in isolation. There may be a host of other organizations, professional groups and academics also working within the health sector to address the same priority areas.

Whether the health promotion objectives of a state or country relate to tobacco control, physical activity promotion, nutrition education, alcohol education, school health education or AIDS education, the new health agency is unlikely to be solely responsible or accountable for achieving them. These issues need to be tackled using a 'whole of government, whole of community' approach, and it is the role of the agency to support and encourage participation of the different players.

Similarly, if success is achieved in measuring a reduction in health-harming behaviours at the population level after a number of years, it will not be possible to separate the specific contribution of the funding organization from the contributions of other parts of the public health system or other government departments or NGOs which may have collaborated.

5.2.2 Time taken for change

A number of studies in the scientific literature have concluded that achieving measurable changes simply in the prevalence of risk factors, such as smoking, requires considerable time, possibly 10 to 20 years of sustained and adequately resourced activities, in order to yield outcomes on a mass scale.[49] Such limitations may be even more significant given the fact that new agencies, particularly those in developing countries, face many challenges, such as limited infrastructure and a lack of skills to implement health promotion in the community.

Demonstrating measurable changes in morbidity and mortality is even more difficult, given that these are further away from health promotion action than behavioural risk factors. Achieving such changes may require a considerably longer time-frame and will be affected by many other factors beyond the influence of an organization.[50]

It is proposed, therefore, that an evaluation framework should emphasize the importance of measuring at a level that is practical to evaluate. There is a need to identify short- and medium-term indicators and to use process and impact measures. It is suggested that these will provide a more realistic measure of organizations' effectiveness.[51]

5.2.3 External versus internal evaluation

One of the issues to be addressed is who should conduct the evaluation of the organization and its programmes: an external group, the organization itself or a combination of the two?

[49] Holman CDJ, Donovan RJ, Corti B. *Op cit*. Ref 15.
[50] Nutbeam D. Evaluating health promotion: progress, problems and solutions. *Health Promotion International*. 1998, 13: 27-44.
[51] Holman CDJ, Donovan RJ, Corti B. *Op cit*. Ref 15: 63.

External

An external organization will be perceived to be independent. If based in a university, it will be able to gather expertise from a range of faculties and is more likely to publish results than if located within the funding agency. If, however, it keeps at complete arms length from the funding agency and merely provides reports, there may be lost opportunities for discussion and debate about results and the provision of advice or suggestions about how problem areas may be addressed.

This option may also prove very expensive, particularly if the external group is responsible for the day-to-day implementation of the evaluation and the collation of the statistical data. In some countries, this approach may not be feasible as the necessary evaluation expertise may be absent within the community.

Internal

One advantage of this approach is that, if the evaluators are internal staff members, they are able to add value by being part of the management team of the organization and, therefore, active participants in refining strategies in response to the evaluation findings. Furthermore, running the evaluation programme internally is likely to be a less expensive option. One disadvantage, however, may be a perception that the in-house option has the potential for bias and may lack academic rigour.

Possible solution

A possible solution is likely to be a combination of the two options, whereby an external organization designs the programme and undertakes specific surveys as well as assisting with the evaluation of major projects. However, the day-to-day implementation of the evaluation system may be carried out in-house.[52]

5.3 Proposed evaluation framework- a comprehensive approach

The proposed framework for evaluation is adapted from the model developed by the Health Promotion Evaluation Unit (HPEU) at the University of Western Australia for Healthway.[53] [54] Although many countries have made various efforts in relation to evaluation of health promotion and health promotion foundations, this framework was chosen as the most advanced and comprehensive that could be identified as being suitable for a health promotion foundation.[55]

---

[52] Holman CDJ, Donovan RJ, Corti B. *Op cit*, Ref 15.

[53] Holman CDJ, Donovan RJ, Corti B. Evaluating projects funded by the Western Australian Health Promotion Foundation: a systematic approach. *Health Promotion International*, 1993, 8, 3:199-208.

[54] Holman CDJ *et al* .Evaluating projects funded by the Western Australian Health Promotion Foundation: first results. *Health Promotion International*, 1996,11,2: 75-88.

[55]Technical and other related reports may be accessed on the HPEU website http://www.populationhealth.uwa.edu.au/welcome/research/hpeu/hpeu

A comprehensive evaluation framework may focus on three major areas, with various strands contributing to the total evaluation picture. These include:

(1) **Assessment of the funding agency:** The performance of the funding body will be closely observed by government, the media, the community and health professionals. It is, therefore, important that the agency is able to report on such measures as the extent and types of health promotion activity funded and the impact of funding on organizations in receipt of grants and sponsorships. It will also be important to report on relationships between the funding body and the recipient organizations.

(2) **Assessment of projects funded:** This focuses on assessing the effect of all projects funded. It may also include process measures that cover how the project has been operating. While all grant recipients should be required to evaluate, the system needs to be such that those receiving small grants will submit basic information while recipients of larger grants will provide more comprehensive returns.

(3) **Population evaluation:** This involves measuring key health behaviours in the population. It may also explore the reach of the agency by assessing community exposure to the programmes and campaigns supported by the funding body.

5.3.1 Assessment of the funding agency

The evaluation of the work of the agency will be based on the legislative as well as the strategic objectives that have been identified for the organization. A number of measures which have been successfully used in order to provide this assessment are: its relationships with stakeholders and partners; the allocation of grants across different priority areas; and the impact of the agency on funded organizations. These latter two aspects are further discussed here.

Allocation of funds

It is suggested that this component should consist of analysis of routinely collected internal data, i.e. information which may be assembled by the funding agency on a grant management system. This type of information is critical for reporting the annual performance of the organization and for comparing activity over a number of years. Measures may include:

- the number of projects and programmes supported annually by the agency;
- the distribution of funding to identified health priorities;
- the distribution of funding to projects reaching priority target populations;
- the allocations to provinces, regions and districts;
- allocations to programme areas, such as research, health projects or tobacco-replacement activities;
- the number of training courses or seminars organized;

- the number (%) of projects that involve a capacity-building component;
- the number (%) of projects and programmes that report the establishment of healthier environments; or
- the number of partner organizations and stakeholders working with the funding agency.

Data collection methods

The information may be collected on a grants management system, which should be able to record data from grant application forms as well as from reports submitted by the grant recipients. Applicants should be asked to provide basic data on an application form which can be readily transferred to the grant management system with minimum input required by the funding agency. The grant management system data files and the application form should contain corresponding core data fields such as:

- the name of the organization and person responsible;
- the type of organization and sector (government, NGO, voluntary etc);
- key health issue(s) addressed;
- key target group(s), age and geographical location; and
- other funding sources.

In addition to this basic information, which may be readily transferred to the grant management system, applicants should also provide detailed information on specific aspects of the proposed project including objectives, strategies and evaluation.

Impact of the agency on organizations funded

This component involves conducting surveys of organizations that receive funding from the agency. Ideally, this should occur early in the funding body's establishment phase and then every two or three years to determine:

- the quality of the business relationships between the funding agency and applicant groups;
- views on the expectations of the funding agency, its processes and reporting systems;
- the impact of the grants on the health promotion skills and activities of recipients;
- perceptions of the effects of the funding agency on the recipient organization, such as profile in the community or public awareness of the organization;
- experiences of introducing, implementing and evaluating health promotion activities; and
- barriers to organizational change and problems encountered.

Data collection methods

A postal survey may be used to collect this information from all organizations receiving grants. To ensure an adequate response rate, it may be necessary to follow up by telephone. This type of survey of funded organizations provides an important source of data on the agency's impact on NGOs and other key partner organizations and may also point to areas where administrative improvements may be required or further training offered.

5.3.2 Assessment of projects funded

All projects

All individual projects should be required to return information which can be pooled to establish a core set of standard descriptive data. This may be completed using a self-report evaluation form. Useful data include:

- population reach;
- educational activities implemented;
- healthier environments introduced;
- resources produced and/or distributed;
- record of media activity; and
- involvement of the target group in planning and implementation.

Data collection methods

Data may be collected using a standard form that is sent to all organizations when they receive funding with instructions to return it at the end of the project. General questions may also be included on the form, such as:

- What were the main objectives of the project?
- Were the strategies successful in achieving the objectives?
- Which were the most and least successful strategies?

This additional information can enable the funding agency to find out more about the process of project implementation at a local level, and perhaps identify some of the difficulties that may be encountered, particularly by community groups that may be new to health promotion. While all grant recipients should return the core data, those receiving larger grants should be required to report more fully on the impact of the grant.

The funding agency will need to determine at what financial level the recipient organization should undertake impact evaluation in addition to submitting only the core data. It is suggested that, for all grants of more than US$ 30 000, an impact evaluation should be required.

Impact evaluation of larger projects

Impact evaluation, to be carried out by those receiving larger grants, as identified by the funding agency, may be implemented through pre- and post-surveys of the primary target group. This will involve random samples of those participating in a programme to measure awareness of the health issue(s) and exposure to the different components of the programme, as well as changes in knowledge, attitudes, intentions and behaviour.

In most cases, responsibility for conducting impact evaluation will lie with the personnel who have been contracted to run the project. In some cases, however, with very large grants, the funding agency may wish to commission external evaluators to undertake this work.

This evaluation component is important because, if the funding agency is unable to demonstrate changes in behaviour at the population level over time, then it will be able to show changes in the main target groups at the level of specific programmes. There is a greater likelihood of achieving a measurable impact upon knowledge, attitudes and behaviour in groups directly exposed to health promotion projects and other activities through specific programmes where the intervention can be clearly described, than in the population as a whole.

5.3.3 Population evaluation

Where reducing the prevalence of risk behaviours in the population is a stated objective of the funding agency, it is very important that the evaluation framework includes a clear and reliable system for monitoring trends in health behaviour in the community. However, while such data may provide important information for compiling a profile of the funding body's operating environment, there is some danger in using them as performance indicators for the agency in the short or even medium term, for reasons outlined earlier in this section.

Population evaluation, if included, is the most long-term of the proposed evaluation strategies, and the measures identified for this level are further from the direct influence of the funding agency than the previous components described.

Community surveys

These surveys are suggested to measure changes in awareness, knowledge, attitudes, intentions and behaviour in the adult population, in addition to measuring exposure to the programmes of the funding agency. The data may be collected through community surveys conducted on behalf of the funding agency, based on independent cross-sectional samples, representative of the populations in the main regions. Community surveys will measure:

- demographic variables;
- awareness, knowledge, attitudes, intentions and behaviour in relation to health behaviours, such as smoking, alcohol consumption, physical activity or nutrition;
- awareness, knowledge and attitudes in relation to risk behaviours, such as road safety, drink-driving or substance abuse;
- perceptions of health and perceived control over health;
- exposure to the campaigns or programmes funded by the agency, such as a 'quit smoking' media campaign;
- exposure of children in the family to school programmes funded by the agency; and
- community support for, and attitudes to, the activities of the funding body.

Data collection methods

Ideally, these surveys should be conducted when the funding agency is first established and then at intervals of three or four years.

For example, Healthway has carried out a community survey four times in twelve years. It has been organized by a university-based evaluation group, with the fieldwork sub-contracted to a market research agency. Data collection involves household interviews in the Perth metropolitan area, as well as telephone interviews in the rural and outer metropolitan areas.[56]

5.4 Key steps to success

An evaluation programme needs to be designed to measure the legislative objectives as well as the strategic objectives of the funding organization. There is no perfect plan that will suit all countries, states and organizations. This section has outlined a framework which has operated successfully in one jurisdiction and which has already been adapted to suit others, such as South Australia and Thailand.

[56] Clarkson J *et al. Survey on recreation and health 1992-1998.* Perth, Health Promotion Evaluation Unit, Department of Public Health, The University of Western Australia, 2000.

Whatever the system or framework used, there are some lessons which new funding organizations may learn from those which have gone before.

- Demonstrate early success if possible. This may be achieved by funding and supporting more experienced groups to implement programmes. These can be used as models for less experienced groups to follow.
- Develop programmes to build capacity in the workforce. Undertake an audit to determine training needs of partner agencies and then develop a strategy for building the capacity of the health promotion workforce. Successful projects need well trained and highly motivated people to run them.
- Invest in a sound and efficient grants management system. This will make data collection and general accountability much easier to manage.
- Develop a system where the level of evaluation required is appropriate to the project in terms of funds allocated. There will be a poor response if the evaluation requirement is onerous or complicated.
- Ensure that the system can generate a statistically manageable set of measures.
- Be prepared to provide support and training for those undertaking projects who have limited experience in health promotion/evaluation.
- Make the development and implementation of an evaluation programme an early priority.

6

The Role of Funding Agencies in Tobacco Control

6.1 Introduction

Smoking remains the major preventable cause of death and disability in the world today. It already kills one in ten adults worldwide and it is estimated that, by 2030, the proportion will be one in six.[57] The epidemic of chronic disease caused by smoking is shifting to developing countries, which means that it is imperative that comprehensive tobacco control programmes are appropriately funded and implemented to control the epidemic.

In 1997, after a visit to Australia, Professor Stanton Glantz was critical of the Australian health promotion foundations collectively which, though funded through dedicated tobacco taxes, were, in his opinion, viewing tobacco as one of the many competing priorities "and not a particularly high one at that".[58]

[57] World Bank. *Op cit*. Ref :5.
[58] Glantz S. Tobacco control in Australia: it's time to get back on top down under. *Health Promotion Journal of Australia*, 1997, 7,1:72,73.

Glantz's view that tobacco tax should be applied in a significant way to tobacco control has much merit. **It seems most appropriate that the new funding mechanisms, if created by tobacco control legislation and resourced by tobacco tax, should ensure that a reasonable proportion of the expenditures are made in a way which will reduce tobacco consumption.** For example, in the American states of Arizona and Massachusetts, the earmarked tax is spent only on tobacco-related programmes. In some jurisdictions, however, the focus is on other health areas as well as tobacco.

Priority health issues may be established by a number of methods, depending on the structure of the organization and the legislative mandate. For example, in Thailand, the Health Promotion Act 2001 stipulates that Thai Health is to run campaigns and create awareness of the harm caused by tobacco and alcohol as well as other harmful substances. Legislation also determines tobacco as a priority in the Australian states of Victoria and Western Australia. For the New Zealand Health Sponsorship Council, tobacco control is also a priority. In this case it is not a legislative requirement, but a contractual requirement with the Ministry of Health. In the case of the Australian Capital Territory Health Promotion Foundation, tobacco control has been set as a priority by the governing board.

In all instances where tobacco has been identified as a priority health issue, organizations aim to fund the most effective tobacco control strategies which fall within their guidelines and areas of influence. Such interventions, which are strongly recommended by the United States Community Preventative Services Task Force, cover:[59]

- informing young people through high-intensity, counter-advertising campaigns;
- informing adult smokers through high-intensity, counter-advertising campaigns; and
- multi-component cessation interventions that include patient education materials, reactive telephone support and proactive telephone counselling.

As well as supporting programmes which are designed to prevent uptake and encourage quitting, the new health promotion structures have a particular role to play in the development of smoke-free policies and the promotion of smoke-free environments. Some are also involved in the replacement of tobacco sponsorship. These organizations, therefore, are in excellent positions to support strong, comprehensive tobacco control programmes, provided that they have:

- adequate funding;
- secure, stable and long-term support;
- the ability to coordinate multiple strategies at the state and community levels;

[59] Centers for Disease Control and Prevention. *Strategies for reducing exposure to environmental tobacco smoke, increasing tobacco-use cessation, and reducing initiation in communities and health- care systems.* A report on the recommendations of the Task Force on Community Preventive Services. Atlanta,GA: US Department of Health and Human Services:2000. Report No., MMWR2000:49(No.RR-12).

- independence from direct and indirect tobacco industry influence;
- involvement of a wide range of public health stakeholders;
- programmes and policies based on proven health strategies, without conditions or constraints; and
- support for advocacy.[60]

6.2 How funding agencies can fight tobacco

Just as the above requirements are important to the success of tobacco control programmes that may receive funding from the health promotion agency, so too are they important requirements for the agency if it is to achieve success in this area.

6.2.1 Adequate funding

As stated in the introduction, the amount of the appropriation which is allocated to tobacco control activities varies from jurisdiction to jurisdiction. While the entire amount of earmarked tax is devoted to tobacco in some states of the United States of America, in other countries, like the Republic of Korea and Estonia, the allocation to tobacco is part of the mix which includes other priority health promotion issues. Tobacco control receives approximately half of the funds that are allocated by Healthway. This includes the funds for health promotion projects and research, as well as those used for sponsorship of sport, arts and racing activities. In 2001-2002, VicHealth allocated over 20% of the total budget to tobacco control while the New Zealand Health Sponsorship Council devotes 75% of its funding to tobacco control through the promotion of the 'smoke-free' message in many different ways.

6.2.2 Secure, stable and long-term support

One of the features of the new health promotion agencies is their legislative base, which ensures stable and secure funding. This means that they are, in turn, able to offer long-term support for worthy projects.

Since its inception in 1998, VicHealth has been a major source of funds for the Quit Program in Victoria. This is a comprehensive programme addressing cessation, prevention, exposure reduction and policy advancement. The Smarter than Smoking Project, which is designed to reduce the uptake of smoking among young people and help those who already smoke to quit, has been funded by Healthway for nine years. Both organizations recognize that any change in the prevalence of smoking requires an ongoing commitment to finance programmes.

---

[60] Lucas R. *Ensuring effective tobacco control administration*. Washington DC, Advocacy Institute, 1998.

While funding organizations have a role to provide seeding grants to trial new and innovative initiatives, they must also be prepared to offer extended support to continue those programmes which are working effectively and which have the potential to make a real difference to health status.

6.2.3 The ability to coordinate multiple strategies at the state and community levels

Health promotion agencies are ideally positioned to coordinate multiple strategies at state and community levels. While they themselves do not generally run programmes, they enable and empower other organizations or combined groups to do so.

As major funding bodies, they have a responsibility to support a comprehensive tobacco control approach following national or state guidelines. If there is no such national strategy in place, it is incumbent on them to initiate the development of one, preferably in consultation with other key stakeholders.

Their ability to overview ongoing activities, identify gaps and then be proactive about providing grants for new projects and research to complement and enhance current activities is invaluable. Such grants may be on a large scale, like the previously mentioned Victorian Quit Program or the Smarter than Smoking Project, which run state-wide campaigns using multiple strategies. Alternatively, they may be awarded to small community organizations to run locally based tobacco control initiatives. Whatever the programme, it should be evidence-based and must contribute to the health of the population, with particular attention given to reducing the disparities between population groups.

The unique structure and place of these funding bodies in the health promotion environment enables them to:

- focus on population groups most at risk (eg. young people and those on low incomes);
- build strategic alliances with sectors, settings and organizations that have the potential to make a substantial contribution to tobacco control;
- strengthen the capacity of individuals and groups to address tobacco control issues;
- encourage collaboration among all organizations working in tobacco control to reduce duplication; and
- influence healthy public policy, particularly through the creation of smoke-free environments.

Coordination has been identified as one of the benefits stemming from the establishment of the New Zealand Health Sponsorship Council, which has provided a focus for tobacco control for the past 10 years. The Council reports that this has resulted in a more integrated approach across the government and non-government sectors, an increase in profile and funding for tobacco control and a more coordinated campaign strategy. The changes have not been due to direct Council funding, but are a consequence of having an organization with a mandate, as well as the resources, to lead the way.

6.2.4 Independence from direct and indirect tobacco industry influence

It is important that health promotion funding agencies are able to distance themselves from tobacco industry influence at all levels. The powerful tobacco industry is renowned for its generous political donations, which may buy, not only access, but also influence among politicians and other decision-makers.

Those organizations that operate at arms length from government have been particularly successful in their ability to reduce the effect of the tobacco industry across a broad spectrum. Through the introduction of creative policies and directions, they have been able to use their funds both directly and indirectly to counter tobacco industry activities.

Tobacco sponsorship replacement

Those organizations that have been involved in the replacement of tobacco advertising and sponsorship in their respective states have been instrumental in removing direct tobacco industry influence on sport, arts and racing activities by reducing exposure of the product. **Apart from the obvious absence of tobacco signage, logos and merchandise at such events, other changes may include banning the sale of cigarettes at sponsored venues and the introduction of smoke-free policies.** Further tobacco sponsorship replacement issues and strategies are discussed in section 6.3.

Exerting pressure to bring about change

An example from Western Australia demonstrates how funding can be used in another way to expedite policy change. In 1991, Healthway stipulated that all organizations wishing to receive grants or sponsorships had to agree that they would decline any financial support from tobacco companies. The four universities in Western Australia were recipients of research and other funding from Healthway and this directive, which some claimed infringed academic freedom, sparked a great deal of controversy within the university sector. However, the universities eventually accepted Healthway's position, recognizing the causal link between smoking and health problems was beyond question and that, as community leaders, they had a responsibility not to promote or condone the tobacco industry in any way.[61] Health promotion funds may, therefore, be used successfully to exert pressure to bring about healthy change in ways other than the direct provision of grants and sponsorships.

[61] Luscombe S *et al.* Pushing the boundaries of tobacco control: the role of foundations. *Health Promotion Journal of Australia.* 1997, 7, 1:57,58.

Smoke-free policies and venues

As part of their grant and sponsorship negotiations, a number of health promotion funding organizations have been instrumental in successfully encouraging groups in receipt of grants and sponsorships to introduce healthier environments, including wide-reaching smoke-free policies.

For example, from 1991 until 1999, when the Australian Government introduced regulations requiring most public places to be non-smoking, Healthway had made great progress towards creating smoke-free environments in public places in Western Australia. The introduction of smoke-free policies was an incremental process, using a 'small wins' approach. Initially the requirement was for sponsored organizations to establish smoke-free areas. Later, as contracts were renegotiated, Healthway required venues and events to become entirely smoke-free.[62] The sponsorship programme resulted in a marked increase in the number of sport, arts and racing venues with smoke-free policies. In 1990, only 46% had such policies in place. By 1997, this had increased to 96% and nearly 60% of the organizations with smoke-free policies indicated that they had introduced them at the request of Healthway.[63] The successful introduction of smoke-free venues, and the wide community acceptance of them, helped to create social norms which strengthened support for smoke-free areas in public places.

This example shows how health promotion agencies are able to add value by increasing health promotion returns on the grants and sponsorships awarded. In doing so, they will gradually limit the influence of the tobacco industry and move the community towards being less accepting and tolerant of it and its deadly products.

6.2.5 Involvement of a wide range of public health stakeholders

The ability of the funding bodies to encourage collaboration has already been stated. They can bring groups together, nurturing partnerships at local, state, national and international levels. Through the provision of grants and sponsorships, they can work with, and develop, new alliances with the health and other sectors, involving them and giving them ownership of the tobacco control strategy.

It is also important to engage a broad range of stakeholders in relation to specific projects funded. The Victorian Quit Program is administered by The Cancer Council of Victoria (TCCV) and works collaboratively with a Steering Committee comprising senior representatives of the major financial partners which are the Cancer Council Victoria, the National Heart Foundation, the Department of Human Services, and VicHealth. The role of the Steering Committee is to provide strategic advice and direction to the programme and to advise the Minister for Health on tobacco control issues.

[62] Giles-Corti B *et al.* Creating smoke-free environments in recreational settings. *Health Education Behaviour*, 2001, 28: 341-51.

[63] Clarkson J *et al. Organisational Survey 1992-1997 Volume 2: The effects of Healthway on sponsored organisations.* Perth, Health Promotion Evaluation Unit, Department of Public Health and Graduate School of Management, The University of Western Australia, 1998.

Western Australia's Smarter than Smoking Program is managed by a reference group comprising representatives from leading health agencies in Western Australia working in the area of tobacco control. These include the Heart, Asthma and Cancer Foundations, the Australian Council on Smoking and Health, the Department of Health's Quit Program, the School Drug Education Project, Curtin University's Centre for Health Promotion Research, and the Health Promotion Evaluation Unit at the University of Western Australia.

It is important that tobacco control programmes and initiatives are supported by all the major stakeholders concerned with the issue. This ensures that there is no duplication of effort, that there is a strong and united approach to tobacco control and that optimal use is made of the expertise available.

6.2.6 Programmes and policies based on proven health strategies, without conditions and constraints

In some jurisdictions, governments or individual politicians may have relationships with the tobacco industry which constrain funding directions and programme implementation options as well as the legislative agenda. In addition, tobacco control initiatives undertaken from within government departments may at times be subject to undue influence.

For those autonomous health promotion agencies which are run by independent boards there tend to be no external conditions and constraints on what is funded. Decisions are based on the cost, quality and potential effect of the programmes or initiatives and whether they fit with the strategic priorities and directions of the state or country. Tobacco funding tends to be placed with nongovernmental groups which are able to be proactive and take risks, and perhaps run more aggressive campaigns and programmes than would be possible in the government sector.

For those organizations that fund tobacco control research it is important that grants be allocated in a way that will produce practical and relevant results that will inform both policy and practice. The VicHealth Centre for Tobacco Research, which has been allocated US$ 300 000 per annum over five years, is an outstanding model. With the help of infrastructure support from VicHealth, the Centre has been successful in attracting significant additional grants from a range of sources for its research programme. Furthermore, VicHealth has supported a number of research projects, some of which examine the potentially contentious effects of legislative change in Victoria. These include:

- The impact of smoking restrictions in public dining areas.
- Young peoples' access to the purchase of cigarettes before and after the introduction of new laws aimed at reducing sales of cigarettes to minors.
- Retailer and advertising industry compliance with legislation banning point of sale advertising.
- Staff attitudes towards, and experience of, exposure to environmental tobacco smoking in the workplace and in the gaming and hospitality industries.

This type of research, though perhaps resulting in controversy and opposition among some interested parties, is extremely useful in order to verify impact and also to inform legislators, health promoters and the community about the possible effects of legislative changes.

The funding bodies must be able to allocate grants without fear or favour, even if the outcomes are unpalatable to the government, the tobacco industry or health promoters.

6.2.7 Support for advocacy

Advocacy is required to place and maintain tobacco control on the public agenda. Advocates give a voice to the various issues that arise and ensure that politicians, the media, health professionals, key decision-makers and the community are all well informed. Advocates will already have played a major role where countries and states have established dedicated taxes and the associated funding mechanisms. They will continue to have a key role to play in the ongoing activities of the organization.

Advocacy is a key platform of a comprehensive tobacco control programme. Where such a programme is coordinated from within a government system, there may also be a place for a nongovernmental organization to take on an advocacy role, as it can more readily challenge the government's approach or perhaps lack of commitment. For example, an NGO may actively promote legislative change, question the monitoring and surveillance of current laws or lobby government members to introduce smoke-free reforms. Those health promotion funding bodies which have identified tobacco as one of their priority areas may consider offering financial support to such an organization. A small, well managed, astute and knowledgeable advocacy group can be a complementary and powerful ally in the war against tobacco.

This section has highlighted the responsibilities of health funding agencies and described how they may use at least some of their resources, both directly and indirectly, for tobacco control initiatives. Those that are autonomous are able to support actions that may be aggressive and hard-hitting while complementing and reinforcing other state and national tobacco control activities.

6.3 Replacing tobacco advertising and sponsorship with health messages

One of the roles which has been taken on by some health promotion organizations is that of replacing tobacco advertising and sponsorship with health messages. For example, in the mid 1980s and early 1990s in a number of Australian states and territories (Victoria, South Australia, The Australian Capital Territory and Western Australia), tobacco sponsorship and advertising were banned and tobacco taxes were increased. Part of the increased funding was used to replace tobacco advertising and to provide sponsorship for sport, arts and racing activities.

This measure, which was a priority in those states for periods of up to five years, was designed to assist organizations and individuals disadvantaged by the removal of tobacco as a source of support and to give them time to find alternatives. So that those sport, arts and racing organizations which either were not offered, or declined to accept, tobacco sponsorship would not be unduly penalized, additional sponsorship funds were made available to those that were prepared to offer health promotion benefits.

In 1995, the Federal Government's legislated ban on tobacco sponsorship came into effect throughout Australia, with exemptions for a few events of international significance. This means that there is no longer a requirement for tobacco sponsorship replacement programmes. However, many of the health promotion sponsorships of sport, arts and racing groups continue because of the positive health promotion benefits they are able to return.

Removing tobacco sponsorship removes a major avenue through which the tobacco industry can promote its deadly products. By replacing tobacco sponsorship with health messages through health promotion sponsorship, health organizations can gain access to target populations that are often difficult to reach and can also work with sponsored groups to create healthier environments.

6.3.1 Health promotion sponsorship

The implementation of health promotion sponsorship is complex and challenging. Health promotion sponsorship is one strategy within a comprehensive health promotion programme which will work best if it is supported by well run and financed health promotion campaigns.

Until the mid 1980s, sponsorship was generally a commercial activity aimed at increasing brand awareness and subsequent use of a product. The introduction of tobacco sponsorship replacement programmes changed that, as health promoters had to become competent in the skills of marketing and promotion. Health promotion sponsorship, like commercial sponsorship, aims to increase awareness of health messages and encourage the uptake of a product, which in this case is healthier behaviour. However, it also aims to bring about educational outcomes and to encourage healthy environments and structural change.

In terms of health promotion, the main sponsorship strategies can be summarized as:

Promotional - the promotion of a health message at an event, such as signage, logos on uniforms, banners, programmes, public address announcements and naming rights to events. This helps to raise the awareness and the salience of the health message.

Educational – the promotion of the health message through educational activities, such as brochures and pamphlets, sporting coaches instructing young players on the health issue or competitions.

Creating healthier environments – This involves the introduction of permanent structural change within the sponsored organization or event venue, such as creating smoke-free areas, provision of shade, providing healthier food choices or safe serving of alcohol.

When negotiating sponsor benefits, there should be significant returns in all of these areas.

Interestingly, when one examines these strategies in terms of outcome and financial resources required to implement them, the promotional strategies are generally the most expensive to mount, while the healthier environments are less costly and have the potential to create permanent, healthy environmental change.

The main focus for those involved in health sponsorship is the target audience. Regardless of the type of event, it is important to determine the nature of the target audience, its health risk factors and its levels of social and economic disadvantage to assess the potential health promotion value of the sponsorship.[64]

6.3.2 Legislative considerations for tobacco sponsorship replacement

If governments are to use some of the dedicated tobacco taxes to replace tobacco advertising and sponsorship, there are a number of issues which must be addressed within legislation. Such legislation may also include a broader range of provisions designed to curb the promotion, marketing and availability of tobacco products.[65]

Before starting to prepare legislation, it is important to examine the statutes of countries and states which have already legislated in this area. The Western Australian Tobacco Control Act 1990 and the New Zealand Smoke-Free Environments Act 1990 are excellent references. Appendices A and B provide access details.

The legislative issues to be addressed fall into two main areas and there are also a number of practical considerations to take into account. The legislative issues cover:

(1) the constraints which the ban will place on advertising and tobacco companies; and

(2) the role of the organization responsible for implementing the replacement strategy.

Constraints on tobacco companies

The legislation will have to clarify what is included in sponsorship. It may, for example, proscribe financial arrangements for the direct promotion or publicising of tobacco products, trademarks or brand names through sporting, arts, youth, community, educational or other such activities. It may exclude contracts for employment and services. If there are to be exemptions, for example for international events, these will also have to be stipulated in the legislation.

[64] Holman CDJ, Donovan RJ, Corti B. *Op cit.* Ref15:145.
[65] Pan American Health Organization. *Op cit.* Ref 33.

The Act must also spell out that manufacturers, importers, distributors or retailers of tobacco products may not make any financial contribution to activities, people or organizations where the use of a tobacco trademark, name or logo is used in relation to the activity.

In relation to sponsored events, there should also be clarification that the only place trade marks or brand names can be used is on tobacco products or packages. The use of merchandise and gifts bearing a tobacco logo or trademark should be prohibited. No other article bearing a tobacco logo or trademark should be able to be sold or displayed.

Timing

Seamless introduction of new statutes covering tobacco sponsorship replacement will require much forethought and planning, as well as consultation with the interested parties, including the tobacco and advertising industries. Ideally, the legislation will stipulate an "appointed day" upon which the ban will take effect. A preparation period is necessary to allow the industry, as well as the sponsored organizations, to adjust to the changes. However, this should not be too lengthy and it is important that no new sponsorships can be entered into during this time.

The role of the organization responsible for the replacement strategy

The legislation will be required to spell out precisely how the sponsorship or advertising replacement business is to be managed. A responsible organization should be nominated within the statute. The objectives of such an organization will include the ability to offer an alternative source of funds to organizations currently supported by the manufacturers or wholesalers of tobacco.

Reference should be made to the requirement of the administering organization to promote health and healthy lifestyles as part of the sponsorship replacement strategy. This means there is an obligation on the sport, arts or racing organization accepting the funds to provide health promotion returns.

There will generally be a time-limit placed on the period of priority for tobacco sponsorship and advertising replacement, perhaps up to five years. It may be included as a legislative requirement that organizations seeking replacement sponsorship have to produce evidence that they have tried to attract alternative sponsorship before being considered eligible.

The legislation will also indicate the proportion of funds, or perhaps a minimum or maximum amount, which is to be used for the purpose of tobacco sponsorship replacement.

The person or body responsible for enforcement of the provisions of the Act must also be identified within the legislation. Penalties for breaches must also be stipulated.

6.3.3 Practical considerations when replacing tobacco sponsorship

While the legislation must be comprehensive and cover all loopholes, it is equally important to prepare for the many practical issues which will be confronted in the early days of a tobacco sponsorship replacement programme. The area of tobacco sponsorship and advertising replacement has the potential to become difficult and contentious. It generally involves a major change to the secure and comfortable arrangements enjoyed by both the tobacco companies and the sponsored groups and the breaking up of often long-term and mutually beneficial partnerships. The change will most probably have been opposed by the tobacco industry, which may have gained support for its stance from the sponsored groups.

The change in funding sources may engender uncertainty and fear as the sponsored groups are forced to do business with unknown and unproven health agencies, most of which will have limited experience working in the field of sponsorship. **Successful sponsorships require the building of relationships, founded on trust and respect, between the sponsored organization and the sponsor (the group which offers the funds in return for benefits). This takes time, effort and commitment from both parties.**

In the beginning, however, there are numerous pressing issues which will impact on the success of the replacement strategy and many questions which will need to be answered before the strategy can be completed. Common questions include:

- *How will we estimate how much money is needed to buy out the tobacco sponsorships?*

  This is difficult to assess. The tobacco industry is likely to claim that the funds required will amount to much more than the funding organization can afford. However, a proportion of tobacco industry funds tends to be spent on extraneous activities like entertainment or providing tickets. The replacement funds should only cover those paid directly to the sport, arts or racing organizations. Where tobacco sponsorship has been successfully replaced in the past, the amount required was generally lower than that which was quoted by the tobacco industry prior to the introduction of legislation.

  It may be appropriate for the legislation to enable a buy-out of sponsorship or advertising in stages, so that priority areas can be actioned first. This may only continue for a few years while alternative sponsorship is found, and, when funds are no longer needed in those initial priority areas, they can be used for buy-outs in other areas. So that this remains manageable, it is very important that the legislation prevents tobacco companies from undertaking new or additional sponsorships during any period of transition.

- *Will the contract be bought out for the remaining period of the tobacco contract, which may be up to five years, or will there be a staged buy-out… for example, two years followed by three?*

  The latter is the preferable option as there is more control over the contract and the performance of the sponsored group. In addition, this approach provides an opportunity for the health promotion benefits to be renegotiated as the buy-out period extends.

- *How will commensurate health promotion gains be achieved for the funds spent on the buy-out? Will the health promotion message reach the same exposure and prominence as tobacco did?*

  It is important that the funding is not regarded as a grant or hand-out, and that it is treated as a sponsorship for which benefits must be returned. The sponsorship agreement must specify any requirements or conditions that those involved in the sponsorship must fulfil, including addressing the standard of behaviour expected of players and teams to ensure that the health message is not compromised.

- *Does the health promotion sponsorship have to be allocated to the same activities as the tobacco sponsorship?*

  Not necessarily. For example, if a sporting organization receives US$ 50 000 per year from a tobacco company to organize a lavish dinner at which awards are presented, this may not be considered an appropriate health-promoting event. The new sponsorship can offer the same amount, but to be used for junior development, coaching programmes or other more suitable activities.

- *Can there be confidence that the contracts presented for replacement consideration are of the same financial value and duration as previously in place with the tobacco industry. Do they offer equivalent benefits?*

  There is a danger that unscrupulous operators, perhaps in collusion with the tobacco industry, may alter the contractual terms and conditions for additional gain. Organizations may also try to sell off the tobacco package to another sponsor and leave the health agency with limited opportunity to capitalize on the sponsorship.

  Sport, arts and racing organizations need to feel confident that, with legislative support, their replacement funds will be secure. The board members, directors and staff of the organization responsible for the replacement strategy will be the ones to sell this message and, in doing so, will begin to form positive and trusting relationships with the groups.

  It is also important to stress to the organizations that, by accepting and embracing health promotion sponsorship, they are taking steps which will bring long-term health benefits to their participants, members and spectators.

- *If major popular sports like soccer are readily able to find alternative sources of sponsorship to replace tobacco, will this leave the health agency with the less desirable and lower profile sports for sponsorship, and does this matter?*

  This is not a major concern. To gain optimal advantage from high profile sport sponsorship, it is necessary to invest a great deal of money in promotional activities, and this may be out of reach for the replacement organization. There is great value in involvement in community-based or grass-roots activities which provide excellent opportunities for health education and the introduction of healthier environments.

- *Will sponsorship funds only be directed to those organizations that had tobacco sponsorship in the past? If so, is it fair and equitable that those who took 'dirty' money from tobacco are rewarded, while those groups who declined or were not offered tobacco sponsorship miss out yet again?*

  In jurisdictions where tobacco sponsorship has been replaced, funds are also generally made available for those groups which did not have tobacco sponsorship and which have the potential to strongly promote health messages.

- *Is it possible to emulate the tobacco industry or other commercial sponsors who are able to support their sponsorships with many additional forms of promotion, including costly advertising, sales promotions, publicity and public relations, promotional gifts and free samples?*

  While health agencies may not be able to compete financially or commercially, they can be a formidable presence in the sponsorship arena using limited promotional and expansive educational strategies as well as working towards healthier environments.

Responses to these questions need to be framed in terms of the requirements and intention of the legislation.

In this non-traditional area, health promoters operate in a commercial and social environment using taxpayers' money to achieve their ends. Openness, accountability and ensuring value for money are as important here as in all other health promotion endeavours.

While there may be many difficult and challenging issues to tackle, the replacement of tobacco advertising and sponsorship has proven to be very effective in terms of health promotion returns, as has been found in an evaluation of the Western Australian programme. The benefits are summarized below:[66]

- Venues where tobacco sponsorship was replaced attracted those with high-risk behaviours. They provided a way to access 'hard-to-reach' groups.
- The venues produced sustainable healthy changes, including the introduction of smoke-free policies, which were included in the conditions for sponsorship.
- New health-promoting partnerships were developed.
- Most importantly, the disappearance of tobacco sponsorship meant that children and adults were no longer exposed to the promotion of tobacco.

[66] Holman CDJ *et al.* Banning tobacco sponsorship: replacing tobacco with health messages and creating health promoting environments. *Tobacco Control* ,1997, 6, 2:115-121.

7 Conclusions

This report provides an overview of how some countries and states have successfully established dedicated taxes, mainly sourced from tobacco, and applied them to health promotion/ tobacco control programmes. A number of organizational models to administer the taxes are described, with examples cited of how they have been developed and progressed in various states and countries. The report also includes a framework for evaluation of the work of such organizations, an important and complex task given that they administer significant funds which are allocated to a range of diverse organizations and activities. Finally, there is a focus on tobacco control and what can be achieved by the funding bodies in this crucial area which remains the major preventable cause of death and disease in the world today. In collating the experiences of a number of countries which have already implemented dedicated taxes and established appropriate funding mechanisms, the report aims to provide a blueprint for other jurisdictions wishing to take action.

Now is the time to act

There are a number of compelling reasons why now is the time to act.

The WHO Framework Convention on Tobacco Control (FCTC) marks a new era in global tobacco control. It provides a framework for tobacco control measures to be implemented at national, regional and international levels in order to reduce the prevalence of smoking and exposure to tobacco smoke.[67] These include: implementing tax and, where appropriate, price policies on tobacco products in order to reduce consumption; banning all tobacco advertising, promotion and sponsorship; and promoting broad access to effective and comprehensive educational and public awareness tobacco control programmes. Simply by raising tobacco taxes and dedicating all or part of them to tobacco control/ health promotion programmes, even the poorest of countries can honour their obligations in relation to the FCTC.

[67] World Health Assembly, *Op cit.*1.

The deaths and disability caused by tobacco are entirely preventable. Predictions present a dire picture. Today about one in three people smokes and this translates to 1.2 billion adults. By 2025, this will rise to 1.64 billion people, and around one in six of them will die because they smoked. Action to address this worsening global health crisis must be taken now.[68] [69]

We know what works. Comprehensive tobacco control will not reduce taxes collected nor result in job losses. Tobacco control measures which cover price increases, advertising bans, smoke-free environments, and education and public awareness campaigns are effective in terms of health and cost in both industrialized and developing countries.

States and countries have every reason to act now to address the harm caused by tobacco. By increasing taxes and dedicating all or part of that increase to health promotion/ tobacco control activities they also have the means with which to act.

[68] Mackay J. The tobacco epidemic: some future scenarios. *Development Bulletin*, 2001, 54:21.
[69] World Bank, *Op cit.*, Ref 5:1.

APPENDICES

APPENDIX A:

Examples of states and countries which have dedicated tobacco taxes and the organizational structures established to administer the funds for health promotion and tobacco control

Model 1- Health promotion foundation
Model 2- Unit within government department
Model 3- Composite model

For further discussion of the organizational structures/models see section 4.3.

State/Country	Organization & funding model	Legislation	Funding sources	Amount	Population	Purposes of the act/fund
AUSTRALIA Australian Capital Territory	Healthpact www.health.act.gov.au/healthpact/ Model 1	Health Promotion Act 1995 www.legislation.act.gov.au	*Formerly tobacco-now consolidated revenue	US$ 1.4 million	300 000	Fund activities related to the promotion of good health, promote good health in the community through the sponsorship of sports, recreation, arts and cultural activities.

* Pre 1997. In 1997, the High Court of Australia ruled it unconstitutional for states to collect tobacco taxes. Since then, funding for the organization has been directly from consolidated revenue.

APPENDIX A:

Examples of states and countries which have dedicated tobacco taxes and the organizational structures established to administer the funds for health promotion and tobacco control (continued...)

State/Country	Organization & funding model	Legislation	Funding sources	Amount	Population	Purposes of the act/fund
AUSTRALIA South Australia	Department of Human Services, Office for Recreation and Sport, Arts South Australia. Model 2	Tobacco Products Regulation Act 1997 (Amended 1998) www.dhs.sa.gov.au	*Formerly tobacco- now consolidated revenue	US$ 9 million	2 million	To increase the State's capacity to promote the quality of life by creating healthy environments in sport, recreation and arts settings through policy development, education and awareness-raising activities. To support health promotion activities with a focus on tobacco.
AUSTRALIA Victoria	VicHealth www.vichealth.vic.gov.au Model 1	Tobacco Control Act 1987	*Formerly tobacco- now consolidated revenue	US$ 16.2 million	4.6 million	The active discouragement of the smoking of tobacco. The promotion of health and illness prevention.
AUSTRALIA Western Australia	Healthway www.healthway.wa.gov.au Model 1	Tobacco Control Act 1990 www.slp.wa.gov.au	*Formerly tobacco- now consolidated revenue	US$ 10 million	1.9 million	As above (Victoria)

APPENDIX A:

Examples of states and countries which have dedicated tobacco taxes and the organizational structures established to administer the funds for health promotion and tobacco control (continued...)

State/Country	Organization & funding model	Legislation	Funding sources	Amount	Population	Purposes of the act/fund
ESTONIA	Health Promotion Commission www.kulka.ee Model 1	Tobacco Tax Act 1994 Alcohol Tax 2000 Health Insurance Tax 2002	Tobacco 3.5%Alcohol 3.5%Health Insurance Fund		1.4 million	These funds go to the cultural endowment of Estonia as well as for health promotion and disease prevention.
FINLAND	Model 2	Act on the Measures for the Recreation of Tobacco Smoking Statute No 693/ 1976, amended 9/4/1999/ 487	Tobacco. 0.45% per annum.		5.18 million	This appropriation to be used for combating smoking, for health education and research and monitoring.
ICELAND	Tobacco Control Board in consultation with Minister Model 2	Act 15.1Act 101/1996	Tobacco 0.9%		282 000	Tobacco control
REPUBLIC OF KOREA	National Health Promotion Fund Model 2 English version: english.mohw.gov.kr	National Health Promotion Act 1995 www.nhic.or.kr	Tobacco (3% to funding, 97% to health insurance)	Overall US$ 8 million for health promotion fund	4.25 million	To establish health promotion plans in central and local governments. To limit advertisement of cigarettes and alcohol. To promote health education.

APPENDIX A:

Examples of states and countries which have dedicated tobacco taxes and the organizational structures established to administer the funds for health promotion and tobacco control (continued...)

State/Country	Organization & funding model	Legislation	Funding sources	Amount	Population	Purposes of the act/fund
POLAND	Council of Ministers Model 2	Article 4.3-9 Nov 1995. Amended 1999 to begin 2003-4	Tobacco 0.5%		38 million	A programme outlining health, economic and social policies aimed at reducing tobacco use.
QATAR	Ministry of Health Model 2	The Law of Tobacco Control- Number 20. 28/ 7/02	Tobacco 2%		77 000	Law specifies a 2% deduction from the whole of tobacco sales taxes.
SLOVENIA	The Health Council of the Government of the Republic of Slovenia Model 2	Restriction on the Use of Tobacco Products Act, Statute N.57/1996	Tobacco		1.9 million	Public health initiatives against the harmful effects of tobacco products.
THAILAND	ThaiHealth www.thaihealth.or.th Model 1	Health Promotion Foundation Act.BE.2544, 2001	Tobacco and Alcohol.2% per annum.		64 million	Campaigns to reduce consumption of alcohol, tobacco and other harmful substances. Health promotion projects and research.
USA Arizona	Department of Health Services Model 2	Tobacco Tax and Health Care Act: Arizona Revised Statutes 36-772	Tobacco Tax (23cents of each dollar)			Programmes for the prevention and reduction of tobacco use, through public health education, cessation and evaluation.

APPENDIX A:

Examples of states and countries which have dedicated tobacco taxes and the organizational structures established to administer the funds for health promotion and tobacco control (continued...)

State/Country	Organization & funding model	Legislation	Funding sources	Amount	Population	Purposes of the act/fund
USA California	California Tobacco Control Program	California Revenue and Taxation Code Section 30121-30130. Proposition 10 1998	Tobacco			Tobacco-related school and community health education programmes as well as research. Medical and hospital care. Programmes for fire prevention and environmental conservation.
USA Massachusetts	Massachusetts Tobacco Control Program	Massachusetts General Laws- Chapter 64c, Section 7 & Chapter 29, Section 2T	Tobacco			Comprehensive school, workplace and community smoking prevention and cessation programmes. Monitoring of morbidity and mortality from cancer and other tobacco-related illnesses.

APPENDIX B:

Health promotion agencies referred to in the report

Austrian Foundation of Health Promotion . www.gesundesleben.at

Estonian Health Promotion Commission. www.kulka.ee

Healthpact. Australian Capital Territory Health Promotion Foundation, www.health.act.gov.au/healthpact/

Health Promotion Switzerland. www.gesundheitsfoerderung.ch

Health Promotion Evaluation Unit. www.populationhealth.uwa.edu.au

Healthway. Western Australian Health Promotion Foundation. www.healthway.wa.gov.au

Korean National Health Promotion Fund. english.mohw.go.kr (English version)

New Zealand Health Sponsorship Council. www.healthsponsorship.co.nz

Quit Victoria www.quit.org.au

Smarter than Smoking Project. www.oxygen.org.au

ThaiHealth. Thai Health Promotion Foundation. www.thaihealth.or.th

VicHealth .Victorian Health Promotion Foundation www.vichealth.vic.gov.au

VicHealth Centre for Tobacco Control. www.vctc.org.au

APPENDIX C:

Contacts

Input to this report, through submission or personal contact, was received from the following individuals:

1. Broesskamp-Stone, Ursel. Head of International Affairs, Health Promotion Switzerland
2. Clarkson, Jo. Director of Health Promotion, West Australian Health Promotion Foundation (Healthway), Australia
3. Cornelius, Margaret. Ministry of Health, Toorak, Suva, Fiji
4. Ewe, Edmund. Deputy Director, Health Education Division, Ministry of Health Kuala Lumpur, Malaysia
5. Gough, Patria. Social Marketing Adviser- Department of Human Services, Adelaide, South Australia
6. Lower, Tony. Secretariat of the Pacific Community, New Caledonia
7. Moodie, Rob. Chief Executive Officer, Victorian Health Promotion (VicHealth), Victoria, Australia
8. Moskwa, Sam. Executive Director, Healthpact, Australian Capital Territory
9. Mouy, Barbara. Director of Planning, Victorian Health Promotion (VicHealth), Victoria, Australia
10. Potter, Iain. Director, Health Sponsorship Council, Wellington, New Zealand
11. Ropin, Klaus. Health Promotion Officer, Austrian Foundation of Health Promotion, Vienna, Austria
12. Sullivan, Denise. Manager of Policy and Tobacco Program and Director of Make Smoking History, Cancer Foundation of Western Australia
13. Vaask, Sirje. Health Care Department, Estonian Health Insurance Fund, Estonia